Transforming the Land & Cities

A Training Manual for
Healing our World

By Sharon Murphy

Copyright © 2020
Revised and Updated 2020
TLC Kingdom Ministries
Colbert, WA, 99205 USA

ISBN 9798559602615

All scripture NKJV, unless otherwise
noted

Property of Sharon Murphy
Please do not copy without
expressed written permission.

NOT TO BE COPIED FOR RESALE

CONTENTS

	Foreword	Pg 5
	Introduction	Pg 11
1	The Lord's Prayer: The Model	Pg 19
2	Our Father: It Was Very Good	Pg 39
3	Our Daily Bread: Removing the Roots of Sin	Pg 55
4	Forgive Us: The Power of Forgiveness	Pg 61
5	Yours is the Kingdom: Decree	Pg 79
6	Sons and Daughters of the King	Pg 91
7	Heart of Worship - Testimonies	Pg 109
8	Activation	Pg 147
	Appendix	Pg 152

Foreword

If you used different laundry products over many years and then one day found something that worked beyond anything you had experienced before, how would you feel about that? Or what if you finally found something that helped you to easily lose weight, would you be excited? Your friends might start noticing the changes and you would probably be excited to share your story with them. Why? Because you found something that really worked.

That is the purpose behind this book. After literally decades of prayer, I have experienced changes in my prayer life and am seeing amazing results and really believe you will experience greater breakthrough too. This isn't a new product and it's not magic. If you patiently read the Scriptures as you read this book you will find that there are things in the Bible that can help you pray more effectively. Prayer is meant to work. Even the kind of prayer where we are joined with the Father just being, not asking, should produce results in our lives that are transformative and healing. I am grateful that I have experienced much answered prayer in my life. But I have also experienced what seemed to be blocks or hinderances as part of spiritual warfare. The Father has solutions in His Word and they have helped so much that like a great laundry product, I want to share it with everyone I know who prays.

There have been so many changes in the city where the Land Team (more in the book) has prayed that friends have asked me to share what we are doing. Toward the end of the book you will find many testimonies and I have been careful to record them as they happened. We have newspaper articles in our files from the past ten years that support many of the testimonies and things continue to change as our region is revitalized. Some of the places we have traveled to have seen even greater changes. I am excited to share this because it really, really works. As you read the following pages, keep in mind we as a team simply join the Father and are led by Holy Spirit as we go. There is an excitement and even feeling of adventure at times as we go on assignment with the Lord, and it originates with Him. We just get to go with Him as His children as He leads us in breakthrough. (Micah 2:13)

The fact that you are reading this right now leads me to believe that God is inviting you to join Him and reveal how you can seriously impact and influence the world around you, like He has done with me more than once in my life in Christ.

In 2006, my husband Tom and I joined the Healing Rooms team in Spokane, Washington and it was life changing for us. Then in 2010 Cal Pierce and the leaders of the Healing Rooms asked if we would lead a team that would pray over our city and the surrounding region. The Healing Rooms had hosted a conference about healing the land and it was decided that it was time to join healing of the land with healing of people. My husband and I prayed and felt called to do it, and we all agreed that it would be something we would develop with the leading of Holy Spirit. It would be called Transformation Prayer and a team was gathered from all over our city that we now call the Land Team.

In 2011, Tom and I were asked if we could pray for people in the same way that we were bringing healing to the land. We believed Transformation Prayer could also help people so we began making appointments with those who were needing breakthrough in some form in their lives. I mention this here because you can apply the things that are laid out in the book to your life and it will make a difference. But I don't include a lot of that in the book because there are many inner healing books available.

At the time there weren't many books about healing the land but by 2014 we had gained enough understanding, and were experiencing God's presence and goodness every time the team met and went out to pray, which led us to share what God was doing through us. After two years we had more understanding, and the testimonies were adding up, so we updated the book in 2016.

It is now nearing the end of 2020 and I am updating it again. In the introduction I wrote in 2014 I made a disclaimer that I was not an expert and it's still true. But I have continued to learn and have found that some of the things I thought I knew were limited by my understanding and what I had learned from others. Now the Word of God and our experience being led by Holy Spirit has revealed some things that needed to be corrected. It has been my privilege over the past several years to teach and train others in what we do. Holy Spirit has led and I have learned through the processes. I have added and clarified those things He has highlighted. They are included in the book to give more foundational understanding to praying the way we do.

There is something important that I hope you capture as you read: God's heart. It is the heart of a good Father who loves our cities, nations and the people who live in them. He desires for them to prosper and be in health. He loves His creation and wants it gloriously set free. He sent Jesus to pay the price for all of it. Jesus made atonement for the land and people.

I hope you will be inspired to join your Father in His heart of love **_for_** our cities and nation. If someone would have told me in 2010 (after 38 years of walking with the Lord) that God was inviting me into one of my greatest adventures, it would have only told a part of what was in store. Getting to know Him and His ways - how very, very faithful and good He is, that His plans and purposes are based on the foundation of His love - these aren't just words to me.

His love gives us the grace to partner with Him as His sons and daughters, and in whatever capacity He has chosen for us to make a real impact where we live. His love is what gives us the authority and power to prevail. As the Land Team and I have found out, when we join Him to do what is on His heart, He does so much more than we can imagine. We do our simple part, and He works in ways that have caused our hearts to overflow with praises and thankfulness. Truthfully, our God has blown our minds at times!

So, it is with great gratitude to our Father God that we celebrate ten years as a Land Team and give thanks to all those who have supported us and encouraged us.

God bless you with His great love, joy and peace and may He use you to bring glory to our Lord Jesus Christ now in this time and forever.

Introduction

What if your salvation is meant to be much greater in scope than being rescued so that you can go to church on Sunday and be nice to others? What if God's intent through Christ's death on the Cross was to bring the rule of the Kingdom of Heaven into your life in every way, with the full rights of a son or daughter of the King and the responsibilities that go with it? What if every Spirit-filled believer were to live and walk in freedom with God and, as His children, bring the atmosphere of Heaven to bear on creation, helping to free it from the bondage of corruption into the same glorious liberty that we are to experience?

I hope as you read the following pages you will see salvation is an entrance into a life of total devotion to our Father and that we are to partner with Him in ushering in the realm of Heaven here on earth.

The Kingdom of God will benefit as we each learn to walk in the Spirit and take part in what He is doing in our homes, neighborhoods and beyond

---

Bringing healing and transformation to our land and neighborhoods isn't something that only 'super spiritual' people can do. The Kingdom of God will benefit as we each learn to walk in the Spirit and take part in what He is doing in our homes, neighborhoods and beyond. If you are a Spirit-filled believer, your life is to make an eternal difference and transforming the land is a strategic way to do it. The people of each city, region and nation may be guided in different ways to bring healing to their land. Nations, regions, cities, and tribes, like people, are born with a specific identity and are created for God's glory when brought under the dominion of His Kingdom. They have particular gifts and even 'personalities' that are meant to be a blessing as they fulfill their covenant with their Maker by ministering first to Him and then to others. The healing of nations, regions, cities, and people groups are important to our Father. He loves people! (John 3:16) *Revelation 22:2* says that *"the leaves of the Tree of Life are for the healing of the nations."* This means that it is possible for nations to be healed, and it is something that we can pray, knowing we are praying God's will.

Whether you want to pray for your home or neighborhood or gather a team who regularly goes out to pray for various places in your region or beyond, we hope this will assist you in getting started. We don't believe there is a need for more formulas or sample prayers, but we have discovered some things that have helped us and hope they will help you. Through our relationship with the Father we have discovered some simple patterns of prayer that reflect His heart, and our values, and give shape to our daily ministry. Formulas are ruled out because of who God is and because of our communion with Him.

Before beginning this journey to learn some keys for healing the land, there are a few things we want to share with you. To start with, we are not experts. We are growing and learning and most of what we have learned has been taught to us through the Word by Holy Spirit as we go. Our team members have taught us so many things of value, as have many others in the Body of Christ. We appreciate their insight and willingness to share what God has given them for advancing the Kingdom.

In *Luke 11:52* Jesus gives a warning.

> *Woe to you experts in the law, because you have taken away the key of knowledge. You yourselves have not entered, and you have hindered those who are entering.*

Experts already know so they no longer hungrily seek for more and yet, God always has more to give. We are not experts and we don't want to be. If you are a son or daughter of God, then you have the same Holy Spirit as we do. It is vital when praying for the land (or anything for that matter) that you are directed by Him. While on the earth, Jesus only said what He heard His Father saying and only did what He saw His Father doing. They are in an intimate relationship that produces fruit. This is the true key of knowledge. In seeking and knowing Him for yourself you will receive the direction you need.

We have found that to try to understand our enemy's ways isn't helpful and can only serve to complicate and distract from our true calling. As a Spirit-filled believer who hears and knows your Father, you don't need to study the enemy's ways. Instead, study to know God's ways. Face Him and turn your back on your enemy. If you know the Truth, the counterfeit will be obvious. As you read this training manual you will find a lot of biblical references noted. <u>Please read them</u> and prayerfully ask Holy Spirit to reveal what He is saying to you.

Most of what you will read in these pages should not come as a surprise to you, but we hope it will bear witness with what you know of the Father and His Word and will stir up a fire in your heart to know Him and His ways even more deeply. It is important that our minds not be corrupted from the simplicity that is in Christ. *(II Corinthians 11:3)* We want to keep this as simple as possible, because we ourselves are simple people and God has blessed us and done wonderful things because we simply trust Him. There is nothing mysterious about what we do, except the great mystery of Christ in us, the hope of glory. *(Colossians 1:27)* Sincere, undivided, and pure devotion to Him and His heart are enough reason for us to want to see the transformation and healing of our cities and nations.

During His life on this earth, Jesus was recognized by His creation and it submitted to Him. Remember His first recorded miracle? Jesus turned plain water into the best wine. He had authority over the winds and the waves whether it was to bring peace or walk on them. On more than one occasion He revealed the best fishing spots to His disciples, and multiplied fish and bread to feed the hungry. Even during His crucifixion, the creation responded to its Creator. The sky was darkened, the earth shook violently, and graves opened.

Most feel closer to God when enjoying His creation. The Scripture in *Psalm 19* tells us that creation declares the glory of God and His handiwork. *Romans 1:20 NLT* affirms this, the creation speaks to us and reveals our Maker:

> *Ever since the world was created, people have seen the earth and sky. Through everything God made, they can clearly see His invisible qualities...His eternal power and divine attributes. So they have no excuse for not knowing God.*

When people sin, the land is corrupted; and when the land is corrupted, people are affected. Cleansing the land is simple; it is not difficult or complicated, but it is spiritual warfare. We will try to give you a clear picture of how it can be done, but one of the important things we want you to know is that though it is warfare, we do not directly engage the enemy. We know that may mean a change for some but having seen the results we can say it works.

As sons and daughters, we have access to the Holy of Holies, the very throne room of God, and are seated with our Lord and King, Christ Jesus, in the heavenly realm. *(Ephesians 2:6)* We operate in the knowledge that our enemy is defeated, and we administer God's forgiveness, healing, and heart as His royal priesthood. Staying under the shadow of the Almighty God as we go, knowing we have been given the authority to enforce the work of the Cross, we have come to see 'hand to hand' combat is usually not necessary. When we go out and heal the land we are part of a 'covert operation' where the enemy doesn't know who or what happened, while at the same time he does know his ability to do harm has been taken away.

As you read through these pages you will first see that the Word confirms the need for us to partner with the Creator for the land to be healed. Then there will be an explanation for removing the roots of sin in the land since the provision for doing so was given to us through the blood of Jesus. We will also explore the importance of forgiveness and the authority that has been conferred to us as sons and daughters of our Father God to carry out His redemptive will on the earth. Then you will learn how you can actively be part of the transformation of the land where you live. Most of the teaching and examples in the book happened in a team setting but please don't think you can only do this with a team, it is part of a praying lifestyle. And finally, we hope you will be inspired and challenged to take your part in God's plans for His beloved creation as you read testimonies of His grace in restoring the land.

Reflection Questions

At the end of each chapter of this manual there are some questions for you to consider. These are to help you process. They are not a test and there are no answers in the back of the book. They are for you if you choose to use them.

What do you hope to get from this training?

The Lord's Prayer: The Model

It started with the disciples' request *(Luke 11:1)* that Jesus teach them to pray. There isn't a record of them asking Him to teach them to heal or raise the dead or cast out demons. I believe the disciples saw the love and power in Jesus' life and they made the connection to His prayer life and deep intimacy and obedient surrender to God and knew they needed it, too. I used to think that only faith was needed as the foundation for my prayers, and I believe faith is important, but it is faith that works by love.

The conversation is recorded in *Matthew 6:5-13* more fully to read for yourself. For our purpose right now He said to them, "When you pray" not *if* you pray, starting in verse 9, pray in this manner:

> *"Our Father in Heaven, Hallowed be your name, Your Kingdom come, Your will be done, on earth as it is in heaven. Give us day by day our daily bread. And forgive us our sins, for we also forgive everyone who is indebted to us. And do not lead us into temptation but deliver us from the evil one. For yours is the Kingdom, and the power and glory forever. Amen."*

This is where we start…*Our Father*

Jesus' prayer revealed His and the Father's heart for intimacy and love. These simple words reveal the heart of God in sending Jesus to die on the Cross for us which is to invite each one of us into His family, His love, and access to all that He is. The word 'our' was straight from Jesus's heart: He included us. His prayer leads us to where all prayer begins: with our personal relationship with our Father in the fellowship of His love, goodness, kindness and mercy, believing He is ready to hear us and help us and reveal Himself to us. The Father's love for our cities and nations is to be in our heart, too, as we join the Triune fellowship of love in releasing His healing and decreeing His heart. God's goodness means we are joining Him, and not the other way around. He desires for healing and peace to reside and reign in our homes and cities. We are able to participate with Him because this is His idea, and when we hunger for His righteousness He fills us and draws us into His plans and purposes.

Too often in the past, we started from the wrong point. We followed what we could see with our eyes and often our prayers were problem focused because we would discern the enemy's presence and became *too* aware of him. It is usually fairly obvious what he is doing: stealing, killing and destroying. Healing the land and transforming our cities will not happen if we continue to focus on what the enemy is doing. He is a distraction and wants to create fear and discouragement in God's children so he can contain us. Jesus' prayer teaches us to start with trusting and surrendering to the Father-heart of love of our good, good God who is not constrained or worried about the things that are happening on our planet. When He is the focal point of our prayers nothing can stop us.

"Our Father in Heaven" magnifies Him and assures our hearts and minds that we are submitting to the Creator of all things and Sustainer of all things, above all powers, and principalities, and spiritual wickedness and brings the perspective we need. He is Almighty. He is the Healer. He is the Resurrection and Life. When we magnify Him, our hearts are encouraged and find new life in His hope. And that living hope becomes the fresh soil that is prepared for the seeds of faith that we release as we pray. It helps us to remember that it's His idea to heal the land and the cities, so we quit trying to convince Him of what He has already done through Christ's atonement.

"Hallowed be Your name" reminds us yet again that it's in the power, authority, and character of the name of Jesus that we have the privilege of joining our Father as we gather to pray. Please don't take it lightly, remember Who you are talking to and Who you have been commissioned to represent. Wear this honor with humility and compassion and grace. *We*

cannot fix or heal or deliver. We simply join Him and do what we see Him doing and say what we hear Him saying. He does the work of healing and transforming and making whole.

"*Your Kingdom come*" is not a phrase that was ever meant to create complacency in us as we wait for the hereafter, but it is meant to create a fire in us for the Kingdom to invade and advance now. The rule of Heaven should bring the presence of the Kingdom into our everyday lives. The Kingdom of God is within us! The goal as we go out into the city or countryside to cleanse and heal the land is to invite God's Kingdom Presence to manifest. When His Presence comes, throughout the Bible and throughout history it means change: new life, peace, joy, and righteousness. His Kingdom of light and life displaces the kingdom of darkness. The impossible becomes possible. Every problem has a solution. Death bows the knee to life. The possibilities are endless as to God's goodness and glory being seen on the earth! Every knee shall bow, and every tongue confess that Jesus Christ is Lord.

"*Your will be done on earth as it is in Heaven*" For many years I would hear this prayer, and even prayed it myself, when I didn't know God's will in a matter. I used this line as a prayer of relinquishment. That sounds wise and submissive. But I question that now. If it really was the Lord God I was yielded to in praying that way, then shouldn't there be a lot more of what is in Heaven on earth even now? I have come to realize that at times I prayed this more from slothfulness or unbelief than true submission. True submission will bring us into our Father's will, and when we are prepared to do God's will, He delights in sharing His plans and purposes with us. We ask and then wait patiently for Holy Spirit to speak to us and lead us. God Incarnate is called the Word and our confident expectation in our faithful Father is that He is always speaking. As we come to know Him and His ways, He shares His life and thoughts and heart with us. Believing this opens our hearts to hearing Him in the many ways He speaks. When we decide we are going to cooperate with His voice and carry out His will, our ears seem to become more fine-tuned to hearing Him. It takes practice and, in this case, practice doesn't make perfect, but faith means we are willing to take risks as we follow His leading and lean on Him, not on our own understanding.

It seems to pray that God's will is done on earth as it is in Heaven, we need to ask ourselves some simple questions: what does Heaven look like? What is and was God's original intent for this earth when He made Adam and Eve and gave them dominion over it? I believe Heaven is filled with God's glory, life, beauty, joy, love, and peace and so much more. We know our mandate as descendants of Adam and Eve was to be fruitful and multiply and subdue the earth. God called the original creation very good and He rested. These are clues for us as we pray to bring about His purposes and plans for His beloved creation. If we want to know more, we ask.

God's Name, Kingdom and Will are the basis for every prayer assignment with the team. We begin with worship and we stay in that place of worship as we go. We ask Him what is on His heart and where He wants to go. As we surrender to Him, we let go of our agendas and causes and give all to Him - His name, His Kingdom, His will. Then we join Him in heart and in purpose.

"*Give us this day our daily bread*" We don't take on those things that are not on God's agenda for the day. Sometimes we think we know beforehand, but we always keep our eyes on Him and trust in Him to give us exactly the portion we need for the particular assignment. Each team member will usually get a part and when we bring those 'slices of bread' together we have a wonderful time of fellowship and our united hearts rejoice as we carry out our Father's plan for the day!

"*Forgive us our sins, for we forgive everyone who is indebted to us*" is key. Individually we keep ourselves in a current place in our walk with our God, knowing we still need a Savior and trusting Him to cleanse us from all unrighteousness as we confess our sins to Him. We endeavor to keep ourselves free from offense and unforgiveness, and count on Holy Spirit to convict us as we stay in the refining process. Forgiveness by the blood of Jesus is how we receive entrance into all the Father's love and privileges as His children. And His precious blood has given us so much more. We have learned to cleanse the land in the same manner which will be explained more fully in another chapter. Forgiveness has become one of the weapons of our warfare that we are so very grateful to exercise.

"Lead us not into temptation, but deliver us from evil" When I lead a training there are certain questions that are asked anytime I neglect to address the subject of being delivered from evil. Most of the questions revolve around ideas that are not always backed up with the Bible but have come through teachings that have tried to explain experiences people have had during spiritual warfare. The questions go something like, "What about the devil?" "What about a backlash from the devil if we begin praying over the land or people? Isn't this spiritual warfare?" "Aren't you afraid of the devil harming you?" "Can you overstep your boundaries of authority and leave yourself open to the enemy?"

In being led by Holy Spirit to go on an assignment, we begin with surrender to our Father, praying for God to protect and cover us as we go, and we ask for His angels to accompany us. Also, as a team we are committed to keeping our hearts and lives free and clear before God and being filled with the Spirit. We pray that Holy Spirit will lead us every step of the way and we have confident expectation that we will be kept from temptation and evil. We are not afraid of the devil and understand that we do not need to engage the enemy to shift the atmosphere and to remove his opportunity to do harm. We cast down the accuser and overcome him by the blood of the Lamb, and the word of our testimony and because we don't love our lives to the death. (*Revelation 12:10-11*)

That last phrase is important. We don't love our lives to the death or as the Passion Translation says, "They triumphed because they did not love and cling to life even when faced with death." During a training no one has asked, "Are you afraid to die?" But that is what needs to be settled in each of our hearts and minds in referring to the devil and warfare. Fear of death has been dealt with through Jesus' death on the Cross according to *Hebrews 2:14-15 NASB*:

> *Therefore, since the children share in flesh and blood, He Himself likewise also partook of the same, that through death He might render powerless him who had the power of death, that is, the devil, and might free those who through fear of death were subject to slavery all their lives.*

This is my question to you. Are you saved? Do you know that the word *saved* is from a Greek word *sozo* that means safe? There are other Hebrew and Greek words in the Bible translated *salvation* and they have to do with being protected, delivered and safe. *Shalom* in the Old Testament also means *safe*. Most English dictionaries have the word safe in the definition for saved or salvation. The point is that you, as a Christian, are one of the safest people on the planet. What is the worst thing that can happen to you? We have been saved from death and given life eternal. I am not making light of the pain of losing a loved one or even our own death, but I believe the enemy knows how you see God and how you see yourself. Is God trustworthy? Am I safe? You have the upper hand in this battle, and you need to believe it. When the Father leads us, we believe He covers us under the shadow of His wing. Even if He led us into the valley of the shadow of death, we do not fear evil because God is with us as our Shepherd. If we truly believe Holy Spirit is leading us, then we know we have authority from Him to go where we are going and to do what we are doing.

In *Acts 17:22*, Paul addressed the men of Athens on Mars Hill as he looked around at all their objects and altars of worship. He said he perceived they were *very religious* or *superstitious* (depending on the translation), which is from the Greek words *fear or timidity of demons*. Let that sink in. Pagans are afraid of demons and afraid of God. They think of God as being angry and someone they need to appease. In general, they believe in a big devil and a little god. Christians have a God who died for us, we do not have to appease Him or be afraid of Him because He is love. And He is almighty. We have a BIG GOD and our enemy is a created being and is a little devil. Let's not forget it. Perfect love casts out fear. God doesn't give us a spirit (*demon*) of fear, but power, love, and a sound mind. If we live with a holy reverence for God, there's no room for fearing demons and we will be led by His peace.

Another question that has been asked is: "Can we make ourselves vulnerable to demonic interference when we are on an assignment?" It can happen if instead of letting God lead, we presumptuously decide we know what needs to be done and do it on our own. The seven sons of Sceva are a good example of this. (*Acts 19:11-17*) They took it upon themselves to do what seemed to them a good thing. They decided to deliver someone who was demonized and even used the name of the Lord Jesus as they had heard Paul do. Verses 15-16 continue:

> *But the evil spirit answered and said, "Jesus I know, and Paul I know, but who are you?" Then the man in whom the evil spirit was leaped on them, overpowered them and prevailed against them.*

How can this be prevented? Ask Holy Spirit to lead you and trust Him to keep you as you endeavor to walk in the Spirit and stay in the Spirit. There are a lot of places in need of cleansing and healing and we often hear from others where they think our team should go, but we keep our hearts focused on the Lord and ask Him to lead us. We may have missed His will at times, but we are His, so we trust that God's grace is sufficient for us if we are earnestly seeking to follow Him.

Let's look at a well-known passage in the Bible about being strong on a daily basis:

> *Finally, be strong in the Lord, and in the strength of His might. Put on the whole armor of God, that ye may be able to stand against the wiles of the devil. For our wrestling is not against flesh and blood, but against the principalities, against the powers, against the world-rulers of this darkness, against the spiritual hosts of wickedness in the heavenly places. Wherefore take up the whole armor of God, that ye may be able to withstand in the evil day, and, having done all, to stand*
>
> *Stand therefore, having girded your loins with truth, and having put on the breastplate of righteousness, and having shod your feet with the preparation of the gospel of peace; withal taking up the shield of faith, wherewith ye shall be able to quench all the fiery darts of*

> *the evil one. And take the helmet of salvation, and the sword of the Spirit, which is the Word of God: with all prayer and supplication praying at all seasons in the Spirit, and watching thereunto in all perseverance and supplication for all the saints, (Ephesians 6:10-18)*

Putting on the whole armor of God is something we are commanded to do and in studying the Greek meaning of *whole armor* we find out it's an *offensive weapon*. That tells us that we are in a battle, but as Kingdom administrators of God's will, we are the enforcers not the defenders. We don't put on the armor because we are afraid, we put it on because we know we need it to be strong in the power of God's might. It enables us to stand against the wiles of the devil. *Wiles* is the Greek word *methodeia, ("method"); traveling over, i.e. travesty (trickery); deceit, schemings.* In other words, the armor is a tool meant to help us see through the enemy's strategy to try to trick or deceive us. The battle is in the mind. Satan would like us to forget that he is the one we are wrestling against and get us fighting people. He also wants us to be impressed with the principalities and powers in heavenly places. But for those who trust in the Cross, we also believe in the resurrection of our Lord Jesus Christ, and that He has ascended far above all principalities and powers, is seated at the right hand of the Father, and has seated us with Him. Read *Ephesians 1:19-22, 2:6* for clarification. We do not look up to the demonic powers, we are above them looking down.

Greater is He that is in you, than he that is in the world!

As Jesus is so are we in this world. When you put on the belt of truth, it goes around the waist, representing your core or identity, so remember who your God is and who you are in Him, and make sure you aren't believing any lies of the devil. Then fasten the breastplate of righteousness over your heart which represents your living, loving relationship with God. Your shoes that have been prepared with the gospel of peace meaning you are under the authority of the King. The Spirit of God enables you to trample out the enemy's plans to establish chaos and turn his schemes upside down; instead changing the atmosphere into an environment of wholeness, prosperity, and health. The shield of faith represents our confident expectation in God. Our eyes are focused on Him and what He is doing, not on the enemy. We don't look at the circumstances or lack in certain areas when we pray but keep our attention on God's purposes and plans for healing and wholeness. The helmet of salvation keeps our mind from being deceived or distracted as we renew it day by day. And the sword of the Spirit, which is the Word (*rhema*) of God, is in our mouths as we forgive, heal, bless and decree, praying always with all prayer and supplication in the Spirit, being watchful to this end with all perseverance.

You are a son or daughter of God who has been given the assignment to subdue kingdoms and to bring about transformation in our cities and nations and the enemy wants you afraid of him. But Jesus has made us joint heirs with Him so take courage: Greater is He that is in you, than he that is in the world! Jesus delivers us from evil.

We forgive through the blood of the Lamb, we then release healing. Then we decree, and those things we decree and declare by the Holy Spirit's leading are aligned with Jesus' declaration, *"For Yours is the Kingdom and the power and the glory forever."*

In *Luke 11:5-8* as Jesus taught on the Lord's Prayer, He went on to share more that helps us in our prayers, beginning with a parable:

> *Suppose you went to a friend's house at midnight, wanting to borrow three loaves of bread. You say to him, 'A friend of mine has just arrived for a visit, and I have nothing for him to eat.' And suppose he calls out from his bedroom, 'Don't bother me. The door is locked for the night, and my family and I are all in bed. I can't help you.' But I tell you this—though he won't do it for friendship's*

> *sake, if you keep knocking long enough, he will get up and give you whatever you need because of your shameless persistence.*

Persistence in prayer is so important. The words shameless persistence almost makes me laugh with joy and it also means shameless impudence or audacity. Do you realize what Jesus was saying? He's giving us permission, and really an invitation, to a relationship of love that has a deeper trust of our very big God to securely know we can come to Him any time with our needs. It is shameless because there is no shame in asking for what we need. We realize we can't make anything change on our own. We pray and God does the work of transformation and healing. Intimate prayers that seem audacious or impudent connect us to the heart of God if we understand and believe our Father is the friend we can go to at midnight, no matter what, and He will give us what we ask for. The parable speaks of a man who was bothered by his audacious, persistent friend, but he gets up and gives him the bread. The contrast is that God is not bothered by us or surprised. He is ready and willing to answer and, I think, He likes it when we pray big audacious prayers because then we get to see big audacious answers.

We need more of these prayers because our cities and homes have big persistent problems. One of the things this kind of prayer says is that we are dependent on God to do what only He can do. We are done trying to do things in our own strength and we come to Him for the answers we need. More than once, we have experienced the God of creation answering audacious prayers for rain where it hadn't rained for months. The weather forecasters weren't predicting rain, but suddenly things changed. And it didn't just rain, it poured. Our persistence to continue to trust Him and call upon Him when there wasn't a cloud in the sky was because we knew we had His heart for the people and the creation. We were bold and persistent, and we didn't plead or beg, we agreed with His heart and decreed what we were hearing as He gave us the bread we so desperately needed. We went to Him as our Friend and Father and He did what we asked because, in truth, we were aligning ourselves with His generous and good will.

In *Luke 11:9-13* Jesus continued to teach His disciples:

> *And so I tell you, keep on asking, and you will receive what you ask for. Keep on seeking, and you will find. Keep on knocking, and the door will be opened to you. For everyone who asks, receives. Everyone who seeks, finds. And to everyone who knocks, the door will be opened.*
> *You fathers—if your children ask for a fish, do you give them a snake instead? Or if they ask for an egg, do you give them a scorpion? Of course not! So if you sinful people know how*

> *to give good gifts to your children, how much more will your heavenly Father give the Holy Spirit to those who ask him.*

As we join our Father to see changes and healing breakthrough, we must trust that He wants to give good gifts to His children, Holy Spirit included. His heart is generous and full of love and light and He wants to share it. He wants you and I and all of creation to thrive. In partnering with Him, we want His heart. He is *for* people. He is *for* our cities. He is *for* our nation. He is *for* creation. For many generations the church been against those we see as evil and the culture around us. Our Father doesn't change the way He feels about people because of their sin. He has already made provision for them. God so loved the world that He gave His only begotten Son! When we have a heavenly perspective, we choose love and we choose to be *for* people and, as His ambassadors, we begin to see things that way He does. And it is good.

We ask a lot of questions and do a lot of listening together as we pray. When we see places in our downtown core that are oppressed with darkness about them, or where sin seems to be happening in one form or another, we question Holy Spirit, asking Him to reveal what happened to give the enemy a foothold? Or why are we seeing this here? He always, without fail, gives us an answer. He will do the same for you.

Don't give up, be audacious and keep on asking because your loving Father has the answers you need and He wants to give them to you. We have been going out with the team to pray in our region for ten years and that may seem like a long time in our "instant" society but in light of eternity it isn't very long. We may not get to see the fruit of our prayers every time but when our prayers are answered we don't moan over how long it took, we rejoice that God intervened and answered!

Reflection Questions

Is there anything you have thought like you couldn't or shouldn't pray about? How does what you have read about the generous heart of our Father and His desire for relationship with you encourage you?

Did anything in the chapter cause you to reconsider or change what you think about God? Or the devil?

Our Father: It Was Very Good

In the beginning God created the heavens and the earth. *Genesis 1* describes a process that began with a formless void of darkness and ended with the expression of God's goodness in fullness of teeming, living beauty. He spoke and the darkness fled as light and order were established. The origin and intention of God in all of creation must be seen through the lens of His ever-loving, eternal goodness. It is the very heart of all He is and does and it is what He wants to see expressed through our lives as well.

Have you ever thought about what our world would be like if sin had not entered creation? In so many ways it boggles my mind. I have pursued God's heart and mind about this, and am sure my understanding is limited, but don't you agree it would be very different? His design originated with the principle of life begetting life, no diminishing, only the power of an endless life. *Genesis 1:31* tells us that God saw everything He had made, and indeed it was very good. God does not use words lightly. Have you ever tried to imagine what the unadulterated environment was like that God made for us to inhabit? When I try, I feel such joy and peace but really can't find any adjectives worthy of God's awe-inspiring, wonder-working artistic expression. It was perfect for human habitation and there was only good planned for generations to come.

Yes, sin entered the world and defilement, death and chaos accompanied it, but through Christ's atonement the curse has been reversed. He has made a way and we endeavor to keep our focus on what God is doing and begin with Him. Creation is groaning for the sons and daughters of God to join their Father in rest and trust, believing Him and His Word. Believing that He is good and has good plans for the earth and giving our attention to His goodness and love. *Genesis 1* reveals a God who creates in relationship and for relationship. In verse 2, the Spirit of God was hovering over the waters and don't miss the 'us' and 'our' of verse 26 that refer to Jesus (*John 1:1-3; Colossians 1:15-16*). It changes our prayers when our basis for praying is intimate relationship with our Father and faith in His purposes and will being done. Too much prayer has been in reaction to problems or only in response to what the enemy is doing which is often just a distraction. It doesn't mean we shouldn't pray about problems, but when we magnify God and what He is doing our perspective is filled with hope and truth. We live in the New Covenant and that means we have a defeated foe so let's quit giving him so much attention and credit and receive the Truth of what Jesus paid for. God-focused, Spirit-led prayers pack a punch!

In transformation prayer, instead of beginning with what we see, we turn to the Unseen One and ask Him questions such as: What was your original intent for this place? Or what are your purposes or plans for this city, state or nation? What is the gift that you placed here? What does your Kingdom coming here look like to You? What is Your will for this place? When praying for people we often ask the same types of things. The questions we ask usually lead to some form of the same answer and that is a description or picture of something that is very good and that has God's underlying motive of love written all over it. When we start with His heart it changes ours. Our motives begin to reflect His, and our vision is enlarged to encompass things that we would never have thought of on our own. That's when transformation happens. Our prayers receive answers and we gratefully realize it's what our Father has dreamed of all along.

In *Genesis 1:22,28* God blesses first the creatures, then humans. We are tasked with being and giving a blessing and being *for* people. Throughout the Bible, beginning with Abraham, we see person after person who God encounters go on to be a blessing and an influence for good to those around them. Abraham was blessed to be a blessing to Lot and his family and those living around him. Joseph is sold into slavery only to be used to deliver the nation of his captivity and his own people from famine. Moses reminded

God that He is the Merciful Father and He listened and didn't destroy the children of Israel after their rebellion. Esther risked her own life to save Mordecai and the children of Israel when Haman plotted to kill all of them. Daniel was a blessing to more than one king and the nation of Babylon during his captivity there. We are called to be the same blessing in our sphere of influence. Like the parable of the leaven in the dough (*Matthew 13:33*) we are to infect the world around us with God's love and Kingdom while often being unnoticed. Probably the most powerful, influential, and covert operation of blessing is prayer. Join God's heart and pray.

As a side note, God's order always brings life and increase, a place to thrive so we should be careful about what we call 'acts of God'. Most of what we blame God for wasn't done by Him, it comes back to man's choices and the ongoing sin that the earth bears. The creation is groaning for the manifestation of the sons of God to arise to our place as peacemakers to bring about God's plans of restoration and blessing!

> *The earth was created to bless man and to yield its strength and fruit so people would thrive and live in their appointed places in peace and rest*

After creating men and women in His image, God blessed them and commanded them to be fruitful and multiply, to fill the earth and subdue it, and to have dominion over the living things on the earth. He was delighted with the creative outcome of His own goodness and looked at everything He had made and said it was good. In *Genesis 2*, God confirmed the authority he gave Adam to rule over His creation with the specific assignment to cultivate and watch over the Garden of Eden. Co-laboring began: the creatures were formed by the Creator and they were brought to Adam to be named. Man was to subdue and bless the earth and the earth was created to bless man and to yield its strength and fruit so people would thrive and live in their appointed places in peace and rest. *Psalm 115:16* states:

> *The Heaven, even the heavens, are the Lord's, but the earth He has given to the children of men.*

Then in *Genesis 3*, sin entered the world and brought devastating consequences and curses with it. Before sin, God walked in the garden in the cool of the day enjoying the closeness of fellowship with Adam and Eve, but then sin brought separation from the presence of God.

> *But your iniquities have separated you from your God; and your sins have hidden His face*

from you, so that He will not hear. (Isaiah 59:2)

Adam and Eve were expelled from the beautiful garden of intimacy and the earth was subjected to futility and the bondage of decay.

Both thorns and thistles it shall bring forth for you, and you shall eat the herb of the field. In the sweat of your face you shall eat bread until you return to the ground, for out of it you were taken; for dust you are, and to dust you shall return. (Genesis 3:18-19)

For the creation was subjected to futility, not willingly, but because of Him who subjected it in hope; because the creation itself also will be delivered from the bondage of corruption into the glorious liberty of the children of God. For we know that the whole creation groans and labors with birth pangs together until now. (Romans 8: 20-22)

The sin of Adam and Eve is described as The Fall. They fell from their God-given place of intimacy and innocence. They fell from their place of blessing. They fell from their place of authority, dominion and partnering with their Creator. What happened to their dominion and authority?

Then the devil taking Jesus up on a high mountain, showed Him all the kingdoms of

> *the world in a moment of time. And the devil said to Him, "All this will I give You, and their glory for this has been delivered to me, and I give it to whomever I wish. Therefore, if You will worship before me it will be Yours. And Jesus answered and said unto Him, "Get behind me Satan! For it is written, 'You shall worship the Lord your God and Him only shall you serve.'" (Luke 4:6-8)*

The word *delivered* is translated *to surrender, i.e. yield up, entrust, transmit*. Man's sin meant that we relinquished our authority to the devil. But not forever.

After leaving the garden, Eve gave birth to two sons, Cain and Abel. Many years later Abel brought a sacrifice pleasing to God, but Cain's offering did not please God. Cain murdered his brother. In *Genesis 4:10-11* God addresses Cain:

> *What have you done? The voice of your brother's blood cries out to Me from the ground. So now you are cursed from the earth, which has opened its mouth to receive your brother's blood from your hand. When you till the ground it shall no longer yield its strength to you. (Genesis 4:10-12a)*

The Message version says, *"you'll get nothing but curses from this ground."* There are many references in the Bible of sin affecting the land and the people of the land. The worship of idols, bloodshed, and sexual immorality are mentioned in connection with drought and famine more than once. The sins that damage the land are mentioned in Scripture frequently, but the main ones with a few references that are worth taking the time to read are: *idolatry (Jeremiah 16:18, Ezekiel 36:18); bloodshed (Ezekiel 36:18); sexual immorality (Leviticus 18:6-27);* and *broken covenant (2 Samuel 21:1-2, 14; Isaiah 24:5)*. Remember Jesus calls us to a higher standard than was under the law. In *Matthew 5,* He addresses the condition of the heart. Sexual immorality includes lust in the heart. And the broken covenant of divorce is addressed as another form of adultery.

We find that most sin is connected to one of the four main ones. Idolatry is one sin that often surfaces in different forms such as fear, self-centeredness, self-protection, self-reliance, self-preservation, pride, and witchcraft. Bloodshed or murder is equated with anger toward, or dishonor of another, such as racism and other forms of hatred. *1 John 3:15* says that whoever hates his brother is a murderer. It is very evident that sin is harmful to humans and it also brings ruin to the land but, take heart, there is something you can do about it!

As sin separated man from God, the earth was contaminated by the defilement of sin and kept from the fullness of its purpose, too. Jesus' death on the Cross bought so much more than our salvation from hell. Speaking of Jesus, *Colossians 1:19-20* says,

> *For it pleased the Father that in Him all the fullness should dwell, and by Him to reconcile all things to Himself, by Him, whether things on earth or things in heaven, having made peace through the blood of His cross.*

There is more! After Jesus died on the Cross, God raised Him from the dead and *Ephesians 1:20 –23*, goes on to say,

> *And seated Him (Jesus) at His right hand in the heavenly places, far above all principality and power and might and dominion, and every name that is named not only in this age, but also in that which is to come. And He (God) put all things under His (Jesus) feet and gave Him to be the Head over all things to the church, which is His body, the fullness of Him who fills all in all.*

Our Father sent His Son to die for us to deliver us so our sins would be forgiven and so that we could be restored back to His original intent for us. As God's sons and daughters, we are to live with Him in us and us in Him, in the sweet intimacy of continual love and fellowship. We are to be His representatives on this planet and, through the mighty working of His power, He has made us His heirs and joint heirs with Christ and given to us, His church, authority to carry out His plans and purposes by His Holy Spirit. We are God's workmanship created for good works. We get to choose God's ways, but the earth doesn't. The earth is exposed to the corruption of sin, while it waits for us to choose to accept our responsibility and privilege as God's ambassadors of the Kingdom of God and to bring His holy Kingdom to earth through lives surrendered to His will. The whole creation groans for the presence of the Creator and for the manifestation of the sons of God. *(Romans 8:19-22)*.

There are many Scriptures throughout the Bible that are evidence of the Father's plan for all of creation to worship and praise Him.

In *1 Chronicles 16:31-33 NLT* it says:

> *Let the heavens be glad, and the earth rejoice! Tell all the nations, The Lord reigns! Let the sea and everything in it shout His praise! Let the fields and their crops burst out with joy! Let the trees of the forest rustle with praise, for the Lord is coming to judge the earth!*

There are many more references to examine.

> *The heavens declare the glory of God; and the firmament shows His handiwork. Day unto day utters speech, and night unto night reveals knowledge. There is no speech nor language where their voice is not heard. Their*

line has gone out through all the earth, and their words to the end of the world. In them He has set a tabernacle for the sun, which is like a bridegroom coming out of his chamber and rejoices like a strong man to run its race. Its rising is from one end of Heaven, and its circuit to the other end; and there is nothing hidden from its heat. (Psalm 19:1-6)

Praise the Lord! Praise the Lord from the heavens; Praise Him in the heights! Praise Him, all His angels; Praise Him, all His hosts! Praise Him, sun and moon; Praise Him, all you stars of light! Praise Him, you heavens of heavens, and you waters above the heavens! Let them praise the name of the Lord, for He commanded and they were created. He also established them forever and ever; He made a decree which shall not pass away.

Praise the Lord from the earth, you great sea creatures and all the depths; fire and hail, snow and clouds; stormy wind, fulfilling His word; mountains and all hills; fruitful trees and all cedars, beasts and all cattle; creeping things and flying fowl; kings of the earth and all peoples; princes and all judges of the earth; both young men and maidens; old men and children.

Let them praise the name of the Lord, for His name alone is exalted; His glory is above the earth and Heaven. And He has exalted the

> *horn of His people, the praise of all His saints—of the children of Israel, a people near to Him. Praise the Lord! (Psalm 148)*
>
> *Let everything that has breath praise the Lord. Praise the Lord! (Psalm 150:6)*
>
> *Then the Lord will be zealous for His land and pity His people. The Lord will answer and say to His people, "Behold, I will send you grain and new wine and oil, and you will be satisfied by them; I will no longer make you a reproach among the nations. Fear not, O land; be glad and rejoice, for the Lord has done marvelous things!" (Joel 2:18-19, 21)*

The fruit of the Kingdom of Heaven reigning in our lives is much more substantial than our salvation from sin. It should affect everything, including the land being restored and ruined cities rebuilt and peacefully inhabited. As you read these scriptures please note that God is speaking through His prophets of a work that is to be done in the cities and on the land. Isaiah talks of a priestly people who repair and restore the foundations of many generations. He prophesies that the ancient ruins and places that have been laid waste by drought and devastation for ages will be rebuilt by the priestly servants of their Father. As you read, ask for the Spirit of revelation to open your eyes and heart.

> *Those from among you shall build the old waste places; you shall raise up the foundations of many generations; and you shall be called the repairer of the breach, the restorer of streets to dwell in. (Isaiah 58:12)*
>
> *And they shall rebuild the old ruins, they shall raise up the former desolations, and they shall repair the ruined cities, the desolations of many generations. (Isaiah 61:4)*

Ezekiel prophesies of God's intent to give His sons and daughters a new heart and new spirit and declares that God would give them His Spirit to be in them. As Ezekiel describes the new covenant, he includes restoration of the land.

> *'Thus says the Lord God: "On the day that I cleanse you from all your iniquities, I will also enable you to dwell in the cities, and the ruins shall be rebuilt. The desolate land shall be tilled instead of lying desolate in the sight of all who pass by. So they will say, 'This land that was desolate has become like the Garden of Eden; and the wasted, desolate, and ruined cities are now fortified and inhabited.' Then the nations which are left all around you shall know that I, the Lord, have rebuilt the ruined places and planted what was desolate. I, the Lord, have spoken it, and I will do it."*
>
> *'Thus says the Lord God: "I will also let the house of Israel inquire of Me to do this for*

> them: I will increase their men like a flock. Like a flock offered as holy sacrifices, like the flock at Jerusalem on its feast days, so shall the ruined cities be filled with flocks of men. Then they shall know that I am the Lord."'
> *(Ezekiel 36:24-38)*

We read here a prophetic word of a restoration that we have not yet seen manifest. The earth is to be healed and flourishing so that people will see it as a sign of God's goodness and turn to Him. It is time for the sons and daughters of God to expect the impossible and to believe that we are called by our Father to fulfill His Word. In *Acts 3:21*, Peter, speaking of Jesus, says,

> "Whom Heaven must receive until the time of the restoration of all things, which God has spoken by the mouth of all His holy prophets since the world began."

A few verses later, in *verse 25*, Peter states that the covenant which God made with Abraham was that all the families of the earth would be blessed through him and his descendants, whose children we are by faith. *(Galatians 3:9)*

As it has already been said, our salvation is bigger than we have realized. *Deuteronomy 32:43* spoke of the new covenant by saying:

Rejoice, O Gentiles, with His people; for He will avenge the blood of His servants and render vengeance to His adversaries; He will provide atonement for His land and His people.

The new covenant has been fulfilled and established through the shed blood of Jesus Christ, without which there is no forgiveness of sin. *(Hebrews 9:22)* As carriers of the life of Christ in us, we have the unction and responsibility to heal, free, and bless the people and places our lives touch. We are blessed to be a blessing!

Reflection Questions

What are some ways that creation praises and worships the Creator?

What are the four main sins that corrupt the land?

Describe how pride is a form of idolatry.

Our Daily Bread: Removing the Roots of Sin

If you have ever gardened, you know that you start by deciding what you want to plant. The soil is then prepared to receive the seed. Often a garden plot that has laid fallow has many weeds that need to be removed. The weeds must be pulled out with the roots so they won't grow back. This can be a lot of work, but it's made easier by keeping in mind the delicious fruit that will be enjoyed later! After weeding you plant the seeds in the newly tilled soil. The seeds take root and with ongoing cultivation and care they produce fruit. Praying for the city or land is comparable. We dream with God by asking Him His purpose and heart for a specific place and that is what we plant. But first we remove the roots of the sin that has corrupted the land giving the enemy access. When we ask the Father to reveal what is hindering the destiny of a place, He usually shows us who sinned. Dealing with the sin before we plant the seed is different than the way we used to pray but has proven to be more effective. If you have ever tried to plant a garden without first weeding the area you know that some things may still grow, but you will reap a healthier, more plentiful crop when the weeds are pulled out and the ground is prepared. In like manner, when we deal with removing the sin and its effect from the land first, it yields a harvest of righteousness.

A good example of the effect of sin is seen in the knapweed plant. It is an invasive plant in our region that was brought here from another area. When it takes root, it releases its seeds causing it to continue to spread. It chokes out the native plants and its roots release an acid into the ground that is like a poison to the soil. If it is cut down it will grow back. The only sure way to get rid of knapweed is to dig it up or pull it out by the root. This is the same with sin, it is invasive, and once planted it will spread and become poison to the heart or the land. It needs to be pulled out by the root, and God knows what the root is. In Transformation Prayer, we keep looking to Him, our Master Gardener, and we inquire of Him to find out the root of the sin. When dealing with eradicating knapweed, it is recommended that the recently vacated soil be planted with a native species to avoid knapweed being reintroduced. What God planted is the native species, not the invasive sin that has tried to choke it out, and He is asking us to restore His Kingdom!

Simply put, as gardeners partnering with the Master Gardener, we find out what His heart is for His plot of land, city, or nation and then prepare the soil by removing weeds and releasing healing into the land. As we declare forgiveness to those who have sinned, it is an act of faith that uproots the sin and its effect. After we uproot the sin that has defiled the land, we, by the leading of the Spirit of the Lord, release healing and blessing, and through the Word of Life, we plant the incorruptible Seed. Sowing seeds is an act of faith and hope in anticipation of a bounty later, planting according to His design by declaration, decree, prophetic words, and prayer. We then ask angels to continue to cultivate and protect what was planted. We weed then we seed! As our time of prayer draws to a close we give thanks and praise to our Father for His wonderful ways!

When the sin is uprooted, we, by the leading of the Spirit of the Lord, release healing and decrees of blessing that were meant to be in the land

---

Do not be ignorant of the enemy's devices. He has an ongoing plan to kill, steal and destroy *(John 10:10)* and it includes establishing strongholds by tempting humans to repeat sin again and again throughout their generations. People are hurt by this and so is the land. When strongholds are established it gives a place of occupancy to the principalities, powers, and rulers of darkness in high places. In *Ephesians 4:25-32* Paul exhorts the church not to take part in various sins. In *verse 27* he says, *"neither give place to the devil."* Sin gives the devil place. The word *place* in the Greek means: *occupancy, opportunity, power, or occasion for acting.* Sin makes a place for our enemy to occupy, it gives him opportunity, power, and an occasion for acting. The remedy is the victory that has already been won on the Cross.

> *Then Jesus made a public spectacle of all the powers and principalities of darkness, stripping away from them every weapon and all their spiritual authority to accuse us. And by the power of the cross, Jesus led them around as prisoners in a procession of triumph. He was not their prisoner; they were His! (Colossians 2:15 TPT)*

Let's be clear: the enemy gets a place because we sin, but he still can only operate as a thief or liar or murderer. This Scripture and others make it clear that he may get access because of our sin, but he only gets away with it because we let him or think he can. The enemy knows what we believe about him and he knows what we believe about ourselves. Consider this: when we sin, it's as if we left the door of our house unlocked and a thief broke in and stole something or harmed someone, but that doesn't mean his access was legal or right. He's been dealt with once and for all. We have allowed him way too much wiggle room and given him far more credit than God has. As the royal priesthood it's time to take action by doing our part to enforce what Christ paid for.

Through sin, and even wrong thinking, we have given our enemy place, but it's simple to remove his access. When we repent by the blood bought power and authority of Christ and the unction of the Holy Spirit, he is done. And that same authority is given by the blood of the Lamb to forgive those who sinned, and that blood speaks a better word. It removes the enemy's authority and access to occupy in a city, region, etc. As believers release words of life and peace, thanksgiving and praise into those newly cleansed places, the result is a change in atmosphere that ushers in more of the Kingdom and Presence of God.

Generational iniquity and sin often need to be addressed in people to bring about wholeness in their lives and it works the same for the land. *Iniquity* is defined by Strong's Concordance as *perversity, i.e. (moral) evil, depravity*. *Sin* is defined as *to miss the mark*. Both can establish a pattern of defilement in a place. Past sin can affect us now. For example, a broken treaty is a broken covenant that may sow continuing mistrust into a community for generations. Often cleansing of the land comes through forgiveness of sin being released over those who have sinned in the past. There is so much more that the Father wants reconciled and restored as we seek first His Kingdom and impact our homes and communities. As children of the King, we carry the life and hope of the Kingdom within us, with an expectation that it is to be on earth as it is in Heaven.

In our authority as His sons and daughters we pull down the strongholds that have been established throughout the generations and remove the enemy's occupancy. There is great power in the blood to bring reconciliation to the land. *Isaiah 58:12* says in the Message translation:

> *You'll use the old rubble of past lives to build anew, rebuild the foundations from out of your past. You'll be known as those who can fix anything, restore old ruins, rebuild, and renovate, make the community livable again.*

Reflection Questions

How does the analogy of breaking off the top of a knapweed plant (instead of uprooting it) explain the importance of removing the root of the sin rather than breaking off the symptom of the sin?

Forgive Us: The Power of Forgiveness

In *John 20:21-23* there is a commissioning of the disciples that is very important to us as royal priests. Jesus appeared to the disciples after the resurrection and said:

> *"Peace to you! As the Father has sent Me, I also send you." And when He had said this, He breathed on them and said to them, "Receive the Holy Spirit. If you forgive the sins of any they are forgiven, and if you retain the sins of any, they are retained."*

Every word Jesus spoke has purpose and power for us today if we will believe and receive. He didn't just commission the eleven, but all who would receive Him He gave authority to become the sons of God. Let's consider carefully what He had to say on such a momentous occasion and how it applies to us as we carry out our Father's will on earth.

"Peace to you" is where Jesus began, and it wasn't just kind words. It is absolutely necessary for us to receive and walk in the peace of our Lord Jesus Christ. As we surrender our lives to His authority, we receive His peace. It guards our hearts and minds, leads us and keeps us and, with peace firmly anchored in our hearts, we become peacemakers.

Then Jesus commissioned them. *"As the Father has sent Me, so send I you."* That is a remarkable statement, worth considering what it says to you and I. *John 3:16* tells us that God so loved the world that He sent Jesus as the salvation of the world. Because of His goodness and love, His kindness and mercy He sent His only begotten Son. How did the Father send Jesus? What does that say to you about how we are to carry out our lives? *Matthew 28:20* says that all authority is given to Jesus in Heaven and in earth. When we receive a commission, it is with the authority of the One who sends us. We have been authorized to go and love the world the way Jesus did!

Then Jesus breathed on them and said, *"Receive the Holy Spirit."* Take a moment here. First of all, as Jesus authorized the disciples to go, He made it clear that they needed the Holy Spirit. We need the Holy Spirit. The fullness of the Spirit is available to us so asking for more of Him is essential. When Jesus sends us out on the land, we need Holy Spirit to lead us every time and if Holy Spirit isn't going, we aren't going. Jesus did only what He saw His Father doing *(John 5:19)* and that is what we endeavor to do. The only way we can see what our Father is doing is by being born again *(John 3:3)* and through the revelation of the Spirit. Also, there is a real need to take the time to allow Jesus to breathe on us and then to simply receive what He is giving us. This is a place of intimacy and creativity in our relationship that Adam experienced when God breathed life into Him, and he became a living soul. *(Genesis 2:7)* Even if you have been baptized in the Spirit, there is a place of refreshing and new life, every time we enter into communion with our Father and allow Him to breathe on us. Receive the Holy Spirit.

In *John 20:23* Jesus goes on to say:

> *...if you forgive the sins of any, they are forgiven them; if you retain the sins of any, they are retained.*

For many years this puzzled me. Forgiving others is taught by Jesus throughout the gospels, but the wording here is different. He was still in the process of commissioning them to go. *"Whose sins you forgive are forgiven"* has not generally been understood to be an act of authority, but when we are commissioned, we are given the authority to carry it out. If we remember that the priests under the lesser covenant served the Lord and administered forgiveness to others in their authority as priests, how much more should we who live under a better covenant have authority to forgive sins by faith in the Son of God and under the leading of Holy Spirit? Forgiving others on a personal level is important but forgiving others in your God-given authority as royal priests is powerful as well as transforming.

Forgiving others on a personal level is important but forgiving others in your God-given authority as royal priests is powerful as well as transforming

In *Matthew 9:2-8*, Jesus healed a man by forgiving him.

> Just then some people brought a paraplegic man to him, lying on a sleeping mat. When Jesus perceived the strong faith within their hearts, he said to the paralyzed man, "My son, be encouraged, for your sins have been forgiven."
>
> These words prompted some of the religious scholars who were present to think, "Why, that's nothing but blasphemy!"
>
> Jesus supernaturally perceived their thoughts, and said to them, "Why do you carry such evil in your hearts? Which is easier to say, 'Your sins are forgiven,' or, 'Stand up and walk!' But now, to convince you that the Son of Man has been given authority to forgive sins, I say to this man, 'Stand up, pick up your mat, and walk home.'" Immediately the man sprang to his feet and left for home.
>
> When the crowds witnessed this miracle, they were awestruck. They shouted praises to God

because he had given such authority to human beings.

The scribes (and in other places in Scripture, the Pharisees) thought it blasphemy that a man had the authority to forgive sins, but please note they accepted His authority to heal. In verse 5 Jesus answered them by saying, *"Which is easier to say, 'Your sins be forgiven you' or to say, 'Arise and walk'?"* Each are declarations of authority. And just as healing is an act that is at once wonderful and humbling so is forgiving with authority. It isn't done out of judgment or arrogance, but grace and meekness. Don't miss verse 6 as Jesus goes on to say: *"But that you may know that the Son of Man has authority on earth to forgive sins"*- then He said to the paralytic, *"Arise, take up your bed, and go to your house."*

The Son of Man is a term that Jesus used more times to describe Himself than the Son of God. He wants us to know that He identifies with us in our humanity. He also wants us to know that those things He did while living among us were done as a man. *Philippians 2:7* tells us that God emptied Himself and became a human. We as joint heirs with Jesus are invited to walk as Jesus walked and to have the same relationship with the Father as He had and even now has. That includes the authority to forgive by the Spirit of Christ and in the same humility He personified in all He did, including His death on a Cross. To continue *Matthew 9:8* says the people were amazed and glorified God that such authority had been given to *men*. I recommend you read the same account as it is repeated in *Mark 2:1-12* and *Luke 5:17-26*.

To paraphrase *II Corinthians 2:10 NLT* Paul said, *"When I forgive…, I do so in Christ's authority…"* Under the Old Covenant the priests were the ones that offered the sacrifices that cleansed the people from sin. In the New Covenant, Jesus's shed blood is the sacrifice that cleanses from sin. We enjoy the fruit of forgiveness because of the precious blood of the Lamb who loved us and gave Himself for us. It is the power of the blood in forgiveness of sin that cleanses the land, too. *Colossians 1:20* says that by Jesus Christ all things are reconciled to Him, things on Heaven and on earth, having made peace through the blood of His cross. We forgive those who sin against us on a personal level but there is also an authority to forgive that we carry as God's children. After all Jesus forgave sin and He said we will do the same works He did, and even greater. *(John 14:12)*

According to Webster's Dictionary, **forgive** means: 1. To give up resentment against or the desire to punish; stop being angry with; pardon; 2. To give up all claim to punish or exact penalty for (an offense); 3. To cancel or remit (a debt). In the Old Testament when forgive is used it means to lift and it's used in the context of man asking God to forgive him and

God lifting the sin from man. In the New Testament, forgive means to send forth. It paints a picture of God removing our sins as far as the east is from the west and expects us to do the same to others.

Jesus brought in a new and radical way of thinking about how we treat those who sin against us: not only do we ask God to forgive them, but if we know someone has an offense toward us, Jesus says we need to go and be reconciled with that person before we give God our offerings. *(Matthew 5:24)*

Matthew 18 addresses offenses and Jesus made it clear that you don't want to be the one to offend His Father's children. He also made it clear that the offended are also the offenders before God if they don't forgive as they are forgiven. He teaches us how to deal with offenses in the church and in the same context of forgiveness Jesus says in *Matthew 18:18 ESV*

> *Truly, I say to you, whatever you bind on earth shall be bound in heaven, and whatever you loose on earth shall be loosed in heaven*

Jesus goes on to share the parable of a king who was owed a tremendous amount of money by a servant who could not repay him. The servant begged for mercy. The king was so moved with compassion that he released and forgave the servant and cancelled all his debt. The word **release** here means to *free fully, i.e. relieve, release, dismiss, or let die, pardon or divorce.* (It is the same Greek word that Jesus used in *Luke 6:37* when He commanded us to forgive.) Then the servant went out and found a fellow servant who owed him a small amount of money but when that man begged for mercy, the forgiven man refused and threw him into prison. The king heard about it and reprimanded the forgiven servant for not having the same compassion and turned him over *(to yield up)* to the tormentors. When we sin by holding a grudge, we face the consequences of that sin. God yields to our choices. We have freewill to choose mercy and compassion. When we forgive someone who wrongs us, we cancel their debt. We release them and they are removed from bondage and torment and the enemy no longer has access whether it be to people or land. As we forgive from the heart and in our God-given authority, we are joining in the heart of our Father who forgave us freely, fully, and extravagantly.

When asked how many times we need to forgive someone who has wronged us, Jesus challenges Peter's faith by responding, *"seventy times seven." (Matthew 18:22)* On another occasion the disciples heard Jesus teaching on forgiveness and they cried out for an increase in their faith. Forgiveness is a true and awesome expression of the

Kingdom. *(Please read all of Jesus's words in* Matthew 18 *and* Luke 17 *for more understanding.)*

Just to be clear, forgiving sin is part of who we are and what we do. This doesn't remove the need for repentance or salvation for the one being forgiven. Neither does it condone or excuse their sin or the pain that the sin may have caused. It does place them where they belong, out of our hands and into the Father's, and it frees the land from the defilement created by the sin. In going back to *John 20*, the forgiveness given is to be led by Holy Spirit, just like the rest of our lives.

The term 'identificational repentance' is used to describe a type of intercession in which someone stands in the place of and represent a person or people group who sinned against another individual or people group. Then you identify with their sin, and you ask those wounded, and God, to forgive what happened in the past, sometimes many generations. In a face to face situation with the people that have been harmed this can be effective because it releases them to more easily forgive. In the old covenant there was identification with those who sinned. *Ezekiel 22* has more to say about the need for cleansing sin in the land. In *verse 29-30* in the Message, God says:

> *Extortion is rife, robbery is epidemic, the poor and needy are abused, outsiders are kicked around at will, with no access to justice. I*

looked for someone to take a stand for Me and stand in the gap to protect the land so I wouldn't have to destroy it. I couldn't find anyone.

The first covenant is a shadow of what was to come. God looked for someone to stand in the gap for the land and He found that someone in Jesus. He made atonement for the land and the people and fulfilled the old covenant. (*Deuteronomy 32:43, Colossians 1:20*) In the Kingdom reality there is no gap, He has removed it, but it's up to us to believe it and enforce it. In the New Testament, when we pray, we stand in authority as sons of the King, who humbly seek first their Father's Kingdom and, in His name and love, release the forgiveness that restores others back to the Father's presence. The effects of sin are nullified; lives, nations, and the land are healed and returned to the freedom to choose God and His truth and love again.

When praying for the land, cities, nations, etc., it's vital to remember that in the new covenant Jesus identified with the sinner and through His atoning blood He took away the sins of the world. We identify with Jesus in His death, resurrection, and ascended life, so when we intercede, we may also identify with others through His love and compassion, and for their deliverance from the bondage of sin. *Galatians 2:20* says:

> *I have been crucified with Christ; and it is no longer I who live, but Christ lives in me. The life that I now live in the flesh, I live by faith in the Son of God who loved me and gave Himself up for me.*

Our identity must be in Christ and His finished work. Jesus charges His disciples to forgive the sins of others. He doesn't ask the disciples to repent for the sins, instead we release others from their bondage by forgiving them in the full assurance Jesus already died for every individual and nation. When we, by the leading and authority of the Holy Spirit, forgive the person whose sin defiled the land, a breaker anointing is released. People are set free, healed, and delivered and so is the land. Forgiveness fueled by love is always powerful! Forgiveness is an act of war. Through forgiveness by the blood of Jesus, demonic structures are demolished.

> *For though we walk (live) in the flesh, we are not carrying out our warfare according to the flesh and using mere human weapons. For the weapons of our warfare are not physical (weapons of flesh and blood), but they are mighty before God for the overthrow and destruction of strongholds. (II Corinthians 10:3-4 AMP)*

Forgiveness is a weapon so powerful that when we forgive someone who sinned we are in actuality enforcing the legal action and court order that has been handed down already on the side of our Advocate (the One who pleads our cause in court, our Defense Attorney) with the Father, Jesus Christ the Righteous. He has already won! The enemy is defeated!

> *He (Jesus) canceled out every legal violation we had on our record and the old arrest warrant that stood to indict us. He erased it all- our sins, our stained soul- He deleted it all and they cannot be retrieved! Everything we once were in Adam has been placed onto His cross and nailed permanently there as a public display of cancellation. Then Jesus made a public spectacle of all the powers and principalities of darkness, stripping away from them every weapon and all their spiritual authority and power to accuse us. And by the power of the cross, Jesus led them around as prisoners in a procession of triumph. He was not their prisoner; they were His. (Colossians 2:14-15 TPT)*

In doing so, the accuser no longer has any ground to stand on. He is a thief, a liar and a murderer so when he does try to take ground against God's kingdom and people it isn't legal, and we need to see him as the defeated criminal and foe that he is. He is no longer the ruler of this world. (*John 12:31, 14:30, 16:11*) The curse has been removed and we have been restored back to God's original plan for us. (*Galatians 3:13, Genesis 1:26-28*) When we, in our royal priestly authority, release forgiveness to those who have caused the land to be defiled by their sin, whether past or present:

> *...the accuser of the brethren is cast down by the blood of the Lamb, and the word of our testimony and because we don't love our lives to the death. (Revelation 12:10-11)*

God has already given us the victory in Christ Jesus and has made us alive in Him and raised us up to sit together with Him in heavenly places that we may know His exceeding grace and kindness. As in every other work of salvation and healing in the Kingdom of Heaven, it is God's idea to restore the land and the work has already been done to accomplish it. *Deuteronomy 32:43* prophesies:

> *Rejoice, O Gentiles, with His people; for He (God) will avenge the blood of His servants and render vengeance to His adversaries; He will provide atonement for His land and His people.*

Atonement for sin is only through the shed blood of Jesus. We are forgiven, cleansed, and redeemed from sin and healed in spirit, soul, and body; and the enemy no longer has a place or legal access. *1 John 2:2* enlarges on this in speaking of Jesus:

> *He is the atoning sacrifice for our sins, and not only for ours, but for the sins of the whole world.*

So here we see yet another grace God has given through the Blood of the everlasting covenant. Through the precious blood of Jesus that conquered sin, death, and hell, we are given entrance now into the heavenly life, the redemption of transgressions, and the cleansing of sin in our conscience, and the world. *Colossians 1:13-20* has more to say to further our understanding:

> *He (God) has delivered us from the power of darkness and conveyed us into the Kingdom of the Son of His love, in whom we have redemption through His blood, the forgiveness of sins. He (speaking of Christ Jesus) is the image of the invisible God, the firstborn over all creation. For by Him all things were created that are in Heaven and on earth, visible and invisible, whether thrones, or dominions or principalities or powers. All things were created through Him and for Him. And He is before all things and in Him all things consist. And He is the head of the body, the church, who is the beginning, the firstborn from the dead, that in all things He may have the preeminence. For it pleased the Father that in Him all the fullness should dwell and, by Him to reconcile all things to Himself, by Him, whether things on earth or*

> *things in Heaven, having made peace through the blood of His cross.*

So according to Colossians it pleased the Father to reconcile **all** things to Himself and it was accomplished through Jesus Christ and the blood of the Cross. And all really does mean All! So, the blood of Christ is the atonement for our sin and for the land, all of creation, things in Heaven and on earth, are cleansed by the blood of the Lamb.

God's people have the authority and the ability to forgive sin and the land will be healed

---

Romans 8:19-21 NIV sheds more light on God's desire for the land.

> *The creation waits in eager expectation for the children of God to be revealed. For the creation was subjected to frustration, not by its own choice, but by the will of Him who subjected it, in hope that the creation will be liberated from the bondage of decay and brought into the freedom and glory of the children of God.*

How is the creation liberated from sin? The same way we are - through forgiveness of sins by the power of the blood of Jesus.

In *2 Chronicles 7:13-14* God speaks to Solomon and we see the connection between sin and the land. When drought and pestilence are present, verse 14 gives the remedy.

> *If My people who are called by My name will humble themselves and pray and seek My face, and turn from their wicked ways, then I will hear from Heaven, and will forgive their sin, and heal their land.*

Where there is sin in the land there is often drought, pestilence, and other destructive forces of nature. God's people have the authority and the ability to forgive those who have sinned. When they do, the land will be healed.

There is power, power, wonder working power in the blood of the Lamb!

When we carry out an assignment that originates in the heart of the Father, the land is healed and set free and restored back to God's original intent and destiny, and the inhabitants of the land may live in a more secure and fruitful atmosphere. In the Old Covenant the land was possessed; in the New Covenant the land is possessed and liberated and healed! *Ezekiel 36* prophesies of the new covenant and the fruit produced by the covenant of a new spirit and heart in us, including living in a land with crops that flourish and cities that are peaceful and thriving. *Ezekiel 36:35* says those who pass by will say:

> *This land that was desolate has become like the Garden of Eden: and the wasted, desolate, and ruined cities are now fortified and inhabited.*

The Scripture goes on to say that the Lord Himself will do the rebuilding and that it is our responsibility as co-laborers with Him to ask Him to do it for us; and that in the process He will increase the population, as a flock of sheep, so that everyone knows He is the Lord. Now doesn't that sound like a strategy to expedite reformation and revival?

Reflection Questions

Forgiveness is a powerful weapon of warfare. What other weapons of warfare can you think of that might not seem like weapons at first glance?

In your own words describe the difference between forgiving on a personal level and forgiving with your Christ-given authority?

Yours is the Kingdom: Decree

When we are finished forgiving those who sinned and cleansing with the blood of Jesus, we have removed the weeds and put nutrients, etc., back into the ground and now we are ready to plant. In looking at the model of the Lord's prayer, Jesus instructs us to pray: Your Kingdom come, Your will be done, on earth as it is in Heaven. Jesus was proclaiming, not asking. In my personal prayer life there is much asking, seeking, and knocking and when praying over the land we continue to ask, seek, and knock to ascertain our Father's will. We really want to be guided by Holy Spirit and our asking makes room for Him to lead us in the way we should go. After we release forgiveness to those who sinned and then healing to the land, we begin to decree or declare those things God has *shown* us was His original intent for the place we are standing. At this point we *decree* His will done. As kings and priests, we proclaim the good news of the Kingdom of God that He reveals to us. When Jesus made atonement for the land, He provided for creation to be restored so we declare what we have received from the Lord Jesus, not from our own knowledge or thoughts, but from His heart.

> *You will also declare a thing, and it will be established for you; so light will shine on your ways. (Job 22:28)*

Christ didn't do anything on His own authority and when we decree or declare a thing, we do it in the authority Christ has given us, but keep in mind that it's an authority based on His love for the place or people we are praying for. For true Kingdom authority it is important to align our hearts with God's so that His sacrificial love is the foundation of our declarations. His Kingdom is a Kingdom of righteousness, peace, and joy in the Holy Spirit and our words should reflect those attributes. Jesus' words are spirit and life and truth. Let us seek to flow with His beloved Spirit when we pray.

There are so many examples in the Bible when Jesus and the disciples healed or set people free from demonic possession and they simply spoke to the person or demon and the person was healed or set free. It works the same when praying over our land and cities. Jesus was teaching His disciples about faith and He said to them,

> *"..if you have faith as a mustard seed, you will say to this mountain, 'Move from here to there,' and it will move; and nothing will be impossible for you." (Matthew 17:20)*

Jesus did not instruct them to *ask* God to move the mountain. He told them to move the mountain by believing God and speaking to the mountain. We are made in God's image and He has told us to hide His Word in our hearts. What is in our hearts is what comes out of our mouths.

As His sons and daughters, we partner with Him to fulfill His will. We are His royal priesthood which means that we are priests that have access to our Father through the finished work of the Cross of Christ. We enter the Holy Place as we simply spend time with Him, wait upon Him, listen to Him, and ask Him questions about His heart for our region. Then as His kings we release His heart into our region.

Throughout the gospels Jesus spoke and transformation happened. Read it for yourself. He would say, be healed, be cleansed, go, or even to the winds and waves, be still! Jesus was a flesh and blood person. Yes, He is God, yet in humility He emptied Himself and became a man to demonstrate what God can do for us and through us if we will trust Him and join Him.

In *Isaiah 51:16 NKJV* God speaks to Isaiah saying

> *I have put My words in your mouth and have covered you with My hand that I may plant the heavens, lay the foundations of the earth, and say to Zion, "You are My people."*

God is speaking to His people today saying, "I have put My words in your mouth." We need to believe Him and trust Him to speak to us and realize that our words are powerful. Jesus said, "The words that I speak to you, they are spirit and they are life" (*John 6:63*) and He warned us that we would have to give an account for every **idle** word we speak. In considering the definition of idle (*empty, useless, unemployed, inactive*) it seems that our words are judged when they are not full, useful, employed, or active in some way. Our words are to be creative in nature like our Father's words. We think of prophetic words as being predictive, but in our mouths by the power of the Holy Spirit we need to believe that when we declare a thing it is to cause it to happen. That means we are being proactive instead of reactive, and with the creative, causative power of Spirit led words, we preemptively strike before the enemy can cause damage.

> *For with God nothing is ever impossible and no word from God shall be without power or impossible of fulfillment. (Luke 1:37 AMPC)*

We have experienced it many times. I share some of the testimonies later in the book, but for now let's open our hearts to understand that when prophetic words come that warn of possible damage to the land and people (i.e. earthquakes or volcanos, etc.) we have the ability by the power of the Holy Spirit to do something about it.

Proverbs 21:22 TPT states

> *A warrior filled with wisdom ascends into the high place and releases regional breakthrough, bringing down the strongholds of the mighty.*

If a warrior filled with wisdom releases regional breakthrough, we need wisdom. How do we receive wisdom? Proverbs says that it begins with the fear of the Lord and in the book of James we are told that if we want wisdom, ask for it and God will give it to us. *I Kings 3* is the story of Solomon asking God for wisdom. Solomon said, "Give to Your servant an understanding heart…". And the Bible goes on to say

> *It pleased the Lord and He gave Solomon wisdom and exceedingly great understanding, and largeness of heart like the sand of the seashore. Thus Solomon's wisdom excelled the wisdom of all the men of the east and all the wisdom of Egypt. (I Kings 4:29-30)*

What did Solomon specifically ask for? An understanding heart. The word **understanding** in Hebrew means *to hear intelligently (often with implication of attention, obedience, etc.).* When Solomon asked for an understanding heart, he was saying I need a heart that hears You intelligently, that pays attention to You, and is obedient to You, God. In a nutshell, that's wisdom and when we have it, we are more capable of understanding God's ways, applying it to our life, and releasing it through our words. *Romans 10:17* adds another aspect to hearing by saying that faith comes by hearing, and hearing comes by the word of God.

There are a few things to say about the faith aspect of what we do. Some of it is obvious but bears repeating. Without faith it is impossible to please God, and with faith that which seems to be impossible becomes possible. How do we receive faith? It can come in many ways, but according to this verse it is by the word of God. Faith comes by hearing and hearing by the word of God. There are two different Greek terms for **word** in the New Testament. *Logos* is the one most often used and means *something said or thought, the Divine Expression (expressed through Jesus Christ)*. But **word** in *Romans 10:17* has a different meaning. The Greek for **word** here is **rhema**. It means *a specific word or utterance*. A rhema word can be something I am reading in Scripture that I feel the 'aha' of Holy Spirit moving on, or it can be something I see or hear in the Spirit by listening and leaning into my Father. Rhema has come to me through a dream, vision or a knowing in my heart, or from something someone else says, but it does not originate with me. It is God speaking in a specific way for a specific situation. He decrees, "Let there be..." *I Corinthians 12* speaks of specific gifts connected to these rhema words: the word of wisdom, the word of knowledge, and prophecy.

Do you see how this all fits together if we are to decree God's Word? We need wisdom and faith so that we decree strategies and purposes that are from God's heart. And we receive them by hearing Him, so we are back to the place of intimacy. We need His love.

Numbers 13 and 14 and *Deuteronomy 1* tells the story of Moses sending a leader from each of the twelve tribes to spy out the land of Canaan to see what the land was like. It would be well worth your time to read it now. Let's focus on the "faith comes by hearing the word of God" aspect, the story behind the story.

In *Numbers 13:1-2* God speaks to Moses telling him to send spies into the land which "I am giving to the children of Israel." This part is not mentioned very often when we hear the story recounted, but it was a rhema word, a specific utterance from God to Moses. Long before this, God promised this land to Abraham and His descendants. In *Exodus 12:25*, Moses says, "…when you come to the land which the Lord will give you, *just as He promised…*" in connection with celebrating Passover. There was a specific word given more than once and the children of Israel knew it so well, that they referred to Canaan as the Promised Land.

The story goes on to tell us that ten of the spies came back with a warning not to enter the land instead of moving forward according to God's promise to them. But Caleb said, "Let us go up at once and take possession, for we are well able to overcome it," but the others spoke against going up because of the giants that were there and compared themselves to grasshoppers in their own sight. They were seeing from their own perspective and not God's. But Joshua and Caleb tore their clothes and tried to convince the congregation by reminding them that the Lord had given it to them and was with them. *Deuteronomy 1:26-28* says the people heard the report and rebelled against the Lord's command to go up; they complained, and said their hearts were discouraged by the words the ten spies spoke. The ten missed the rhema word. They looked at what they could see instead of trusting Him who is invisible. Faith is not rooted in the seen, but in the unseen and according to *Galatians 5:6*, faith works through love. As God's children hear from Him and trust in His word, His promises, His provision, and His great love revealed to us through our Lord Jesus, then we will not be like the ten spies who bring a bad report and cause those who hear them to be discouraged and afraid. But we are like Caleb who followed God fully and had a different spirit in him.

> *By faith we understand that the worlds were framed by the word of God, so that the things which are seen are not made of things which are visible. (Hebrews 11:3)*

When we pray or decree a thing, we are listening with our hearts for a specific word from our Father so that we can release it. Only two of the twelve spies spoke from the heart of the Father because they trusted Him and His word to them. By faith Caleb and Joshua understood and believed God's word and came into agreement with His promise planted firmly in their hearts and then it came out of their mouths. Faith brings us to a place of confident expectation in God and at the same time humility and dependence because if Holy Spirit isn't leading, we are not speaking. We believe therefore we speak. When we submit ourselves in humble surrender to our God, He uses our spoken word to bring about His will and to plant the incorruptible seed that transforms from death to life and provides for Himself and us a beautiful harvest of righteousness.

It sounds like this, "I decree…" or "I release…" or in a group, "We declare.." Listen to Holy Spirit, receive what He is saying and fill in the blank. You are a child of God so decree like a king in submission to the King of Kings.

This may feel awkward at first, but it helps to remember that your boldness isn't based on you. It is based on what Jesus did on the Cross. When I decree, I remember Jesus paid for the healing and blessing of our cities and I want Him to get the reward for all He has done. If you are just learning to hear Holy Spirit this will help. Being with others and listening together seems to turn up the volume on His voice. And if you still aren't sure about what to speak, the Bible is full of great prayers and decrees that we often pray.

I decree that God's love is moving in this place and over your heart right now! This is one that always works. I recommend practice in your own home. For example, I decree peace and joy in the Holy Spirit to all who enter here. Decreeing or declaring doesn't take away from your conversation time with our Father, but it's an added dimension to reflect His heart when on assignment with Him.

As we finish declaring God's heart over our city, or the place we are praying, we conclude with a prayer for God to release His angels to help us by protecting and cultivating what was done through His Word and Spirit. We believe their assistance has been a big part of the fruit we see. The Bible gives us insight:

> *Are not all angels ministering spirits sent to serve those who will inherit salvation. (Hebrews 1:14 NIV)*

> *Praise the Lord, you angels, you mighty ones who carry out His plans, listening for each of His commands. Yes, praise the Lord, you armies of angels, who serve Him and do His will! (Psalm 103:20-21 NLT)*

And then we finish in praise and thanksgiving!

Praise the Lord, everything He has created, everything in all His Kingdom. Let all the I am praise the Lord! (Psalm 103:22 NLT)

Reflection Questions

Was there anything that challenged you in this chapter?

Practice asking God specific questions and take the time to listen. If you don't hear at first, be aware that He will answer you. Record one of your questions here and then write down the answer when it comes. It's a great way to encourage yourself in the Lord.

Sons and Daughters of the King

The Hebrew definition for son or daughter is *builder of the family name.* Our identity as sons and daughters of God must be established in our hearts before we begin our prayer assignments. It begins with our trust in Him and faith that He is who He says He is and will do what He says He will do. The assignment is not what makes us valuable, it's the Father's love for us and the price that Jesus paid for us that establishes our value and identity in Him. If we let the assignments define us instead of our relationship all our praying will be based on the outcome of what we can see or do.

Sometimes when we pray the answers can be slow in coming or even difficult to perceive because the land doesn't tell us how it is feeling. We have learned to do our part and trust that God is always faithful to do His. Knowing and loving Him is everything and when we act as sons and daughters our motivation is in alignment with that love! As you read this chapter, I hope you will understand that what you do is to be an outcome of Whose you are.

For many years my husband had his own business. It was rare that we could get away for a vacation, but when we did it seemed there would be inevitable problems when we returned. Tom would go over everything he could think of in advance to help the employees know what needed to be done. We had good employees, but they didn't seem to notice, or maybe they ignored some things, and must have thought Tom could deal with the problems when he got back. But then one of our sons began to work for us. What a difference that made! The first time we left for a trip Tom gave him instructions about the upcoming jobs and when we got home our son couldn't wait to share with his dad how great everything had gone. Maybe even better than if Tom had been home! Our son had been about his father's business because he loved his father and wanted to be a blessing to him while he was away. There's a distinct difference in serving as an employee/servant or as a son.

There are some important Kingdom aspects of the definition of sons and daughters that help describe what we do. We are about our Father's business. We are builders. Usually it means that we must demolish or tear down what has been established by the enemy, but it is with the express purpose of building *(Jeremiah 1:10)* our Father's Kingdom on earth as it is in Heaven *(Matthew 6:9-10)*. As sons and daughters, we submit to our Father's will and work together as a family, in honor for Him and one another. We seek first our Father's Kingdom and His righteousness. And we do it in the Name and for the Name. The family Name. Sons and daughters are not out to build a name or a kingdom for ourselves. Much of what is done, is done in secret, and the family rejoices when the name of Jesus is exalted.

As sons and daughters, it is vital that we believe that God's plans for His creation are good. Too often when devastation comes upon the earth, we hear God blamed for it, and even hear some say they hope it will bring people to repentance. Because of God's redemptive nature that may happen, but it is the goodness and kindness of God that leads people to repentance according to *Romans 2:4. Hosea 3:5 NLT* says that in the last day people will tremble in awe of the Lord and His goodness. What if part of that goodness is living peacefully in our homes with thriving families and the nations of the earth having enough food and clean water to drink, and an abundance of grace and joy because of God's glory being released into the earth?

When we go to pray in a city or on the land we go as worshippers in Spirit and in Truth. Jesus teaches us not to be content with only outward forms of worship. Keeping our hearts turned toward Him as we go means it's all worship. He shows us the way of the priestly heart to worship, to forgive, to live in peace, to be and speak a blessing from the fullness of God's heart and anointing. As our faithful High Priest, He gives us instruction, assignments, strategies, and the strength to carry out His purposes when we come to His throne of grace. As kings we rule over the earth and all demonic oppression to stop the death and decay from sin, and we release the reality of the freedom of life in the Kingdom.

Isaiah 61 describes the good news of salvation: the gospel being preached to the poor, captives being set free, healing of the brokenhearted, etc. Part of the good news that doesn't often get emphasized, or is disregarded as 'only having spiritual implications', is found in verses 4 through 6 which says that the priests of the Lord and the servants of our God shall rebuild the ancient ruins and raise up the former desolations, and they shall repair the ruined cities and the desolations of many generations. Healing the land includes our cities, regions, and nations. God loves His creation and He invites us to join Him in releasing that love. As God's family, He chose us to join Jesus, our High Priest in the order of Melchesidec. *(Hebrews 7)* We are His ambassadors of reconciliation *(II Corinthians 5:18-20)* and royal priests.

> *But you are a chosen generation, a royal priesthood, a holy nation, His own special people, that you may proclaim the praises of Him who called you out of darkness into His marvelous light; who once were not a people, but are now the people of God, who had not obtained mercy, but now have obtained mercy. (1 Peter 2:9, 10)*

Jesus Christ made a way for us and we are now able to fulfill the calling of God's heart as we, His children, enter and abide in His presence. In His presence we, as kings and priests *(Revelations 1:6)*, minister first to our Father and are filled with the Spirit and love of Christ, and then we go out and bring God's blessings to others and the land. A twofold relationship exists: 1) loving God with all our heart, mind, soul, and strength and others as our self. In our relationship with God, we enter the priesthood as sons and daughters because of the life, redemption and restoration we receive from the only begotten Son and our union in Him; 2) and in loving others, there is a humility, compassion and gentleness because we are aware of our own continuing need for a Savior, our Advocate who has passed through the heavens and is seated at the right hand of the Father where God raised us up and seated us together in the heavenly places in Christ Jesus. When we forgive sins in our authority as His own, it is from a place of humility, not blame or judgment. We understand that in the Kingdom realm as nobility we are given power, authority, gifts, and other resources to serve our King and His purposes. Because of God's love we are spurred on to pray so that others will see His goodness and glory manifest in their cities and lands.

As royal priests, we rest in the glory of the Father, we breathe in the clean, fresh air of His Kingdom that brings righteousness, peace, joy, forgiveness, and redemption into our hearts. As priests who rest in His holiness, we breathe out His life, love, and reconciliation to people and their land. As believer-priests we wear holy garments for glory, beauty, and consecration (set apart to our King). We put on the whole armor of God. We are truly a family of priests: men, women, and children. We all have the same Father and our Firstborn Brother leads us into a place of compassion and mercy for others and the creation, as we offer ourselves in worship and praise, then release the love and forgiveness we have obtained from our Father God. As kings and priests, we have a powerful combined anointing.

As priests who rest in His holiness, we breathe out His life, love, and reconciliation to people and their land

---

As kings we have the authority to administer all that we receive as priests in Heaven with Christ. Melchesidec means King of Righteousness and he ruled as King in Salem. Righteousness comes from the heart. It has to do with right standing in right relationship with the King of Righteousness. When our behavior follows a true heart there is good fruit. There are some righteous kings mentioned in the Old Testament and a few Proverbs and Psalms that describe the benefits that the kings of righteousness provide to the Kingdom realm. It is a much fuller study and revelation of its own.

There are too many blessings to mention all of them, but here is a list of a few things that are true. In your identity as royalty you have been given all of this from your Father to help transform the world you live in:

- Worship of the One true God is a priority to a righteous king.

- Safety and security result when a righteous king is in authority.

- *Ecclesiastes 8:4* says "Where the word of a king is, there is power."

- A righteous king exhibits wisdom and provides justice and peace for His people (Solomon).

- A righteous king pursues righteousness and wisely removes the root issues when problems arise in his kingdom, creating an atmosphere for the people to live in peace, rest, and prosperity (Hezekiah and Josiah).

- Righteous kings have a vision for victory through the King of Kings and inquire, listen to, and obey the counsel of the Lord (David).

- Righteous kings fight for and shepherd their people.

- In *II Chronicles 20*, a righteous king (Jehoshaphat) won the victory in battle when God gave the strategy and the king ordered worshippers to lead in advance!

- A true king of righteousness leads through total dependence and surrender to the Lord of righteousness *(Jeremiah 23:5-6)* and in doing so he lives in, and from, a place of rest where our King and His Kingdom comes through us as it is in Heaven.

- I (Jesus, wisdom) empower kings to reign and rulers to make laws that are just. I empower princes to rise and take dominion, and generous ones to govern the earth. *(Proverbs 8:15,16 TPT)*

It is essential that we understand justice from God's perspective. It isn't getting even, or retribution, or us wielding God's punishment. He will repay, not us. Justice is what

Jesus paid for on the Cross. He took all the wrath upon Himself. He calls us to mercy that triumphs over judgement so that we are known by our love and our Father is seen through our lives as the good and just God He is.

Another description of Melchesidec is King of Salem. The Hebrew definition of Salem (shalem or shalom) from the Strong's Concordance is *peaceful;* and it was an early name of Jerusalem. It is from a root word meaning *to be safe (in mind, body, or estate); fig. to be or make completed; by implication to be friendly; to reciprocate; prosperity and welfare; peace.* My friend who is a theologian taught me that when the Hebrew people greeted each other upon meeting they would say shalom which to them meant, "I bless you with the fullness that Adam and Eve had with the Father before the fall."

As God's royal priests we carry peace in a greater measure than the old covenant priests did because of Christ in us, and as sons and daughters of God we are peacemakers. Peace is always an authority issue. If we don't surrender to Christ's authority, we don't have peace. When we do surrender to Jesus' authority over our lives, peace guards our hearts and minds. Peacemakers live a lifestyle of establishing Christ's authority and the rule of His peace by resting in Him as worship becomes a way of life. As a people whose feet are prepared with the Good News of Peace, we walk on confusion, chaos, strife, and destruction, and the atmosphere of true peace is released wherever we set foot. The chastisement for our peace was upon our Lord and Savior and He purchased the peace that we live in and release as evidence that the Kingdom of God has invaded.

> *Seek the peace of the city where I have caused you to be carried away captive and pray to the Lord for it; for in its peace you will have peace. (Jeremiah 29:7)*

The city being referred to here is Babylon, one of the most wicked cities the earth has known, yet God commanded the people of Israel to seek its peace. Daniel understood this and obeyed even to the point of blessing the kings he served and helping them to know the true God of Heaven. When we serve out of a heart of love, peace, and humility, we are our Father's children. When we serve those who don't know the King of glory, we help them to know the true God of Heaven. In his book, <u>Common Prayer, A Liturgy for Ordinary Radicals</u>, Shane Claiborne gives this definition:

> PEACEMAKING DOESN'T MEAN PASSIVITY. IT IS THE ACT OF INTERRUPTING INJUSTICE WITHOUT MIRRORING INJUSTICE; THE ACT OF DISARMING EVIL, WITHOUT DESTROYING THE EVILDOER; THE ACT OF FINDING THE THIRD WAY THAT IS NEITHER FIGHT NOR FLIGHT, BUT THE CAREFUL, ARDUOUS

PURSUIT OF RECONCILIATION AND JUSTICE. IT IS ABOUT A REVOLUTION OF LOVE THAT IS BIG ENOUGH TO SET THE OPPRESSED AND THE OPPRESSOR FREE.

From this place of intimate love we carry His authority and anointing. God's true authority and anointing are given for the purpose of service in our Father's Kingdom. In *Hebrews 7:25* we see that our High Priest Jesus always lives to intercede for us. The intercession of Jesus is revealed as a laying down of His life for us and He calls us to do the same: *"If My people…"! (2 Chronicles 7:14)* We choose to humble ourselves and pray and seek His face and turn from our own ways and the sin that would try to entangle us. We lay down our lives for our King in total devotion and surrender wearing humility as a cloak over our armor. True humility knows and believes who God is and what He can do. When we humble ourselves it means we agree with who God says we are. Humility of mind may also be described as flexibility, teachability and courage to try new things as we trust in the Lord's grace to help us correct course if we do err. Like Jesus we go into the Holy of Holies and see and hear what our Father is doing and with a heart of compassion like His, we declare it.

Humility does not judge or blame those who have sinned, we simply forgive and release them; we stand in the gap with our

Lord in service to Him, and the people of the land, cities, and nations. Instead of blaming someone (or anyone) for our condition we take responsibility as God's people and believe His Word. We do not want to be ignorant of the enemy's way of doing things - according to *Revelation 12:10* he *accuses*: *to blame, find fault, or to bring formal charges against, as a plaintiff or prosecuting attorney.* He wants to snare us into captivity, make us prisoners of war and to take advantage of us. He is already defeated but sin allows him to condemn and do harm. The accusations he speaks often originate with those who have power and authority in the Kingdom: God's sons and daughters. Idle words of criticism, gossip, strife, judgment, malice, etc., are harmful and are used to do the enemy's will.

As the accuser of the Church the enemy uses blame as one of his chief weapons. He gets an advantage when we fall for his devices. If we blame someone for our condition, or the condition of our city or nation, we become a victim of that person. When we think like a victim, we usually become resentful and in a way that we don't always realize. When we are resentful, we spend time thinking and rethinking and sometimes building a case against the person. By doing that, we give that person undue influence. We might not consciously realize it but we have made them more powerful than God, and what God in His grace can do when we trust

Him. That person has now become an idol in our life. Not only that, when I, as a child of God, His delegate on earth to bring about righteousness, peace, and joy, blame a person, I am forgetting who the true enemy is. When we choose to forgive someone's sin instead of blaming them, we ask God how He sees them and declare the truth over them. Otherwise, our unforgiveness and blame not only keeps us stuck, but it has the potential to keep them stuck, too. So, our call is not to blame but to go out and release forgiveness as His children of grace. This is important because "victim" thinking can affect us in so many ways, including how we pray. Instead of being specific and powerful, our prayers become generalized and self-centered asking for deliverance instead of giving it.

When people sin and the land is defiled it opens doors to the enemy to kill, steal, and destroy. But we, like Abraham, Moses, Esther, Ezekiel, and many others *(Genesis 18:22-33, Numbers 14:11-20, Esther 4:14)*, stand for mercy. We forgive those who sinned because we know that God wants all to come to repentance and to know Him. We stand in love, gratitude, and humility because we have been forgiven through the blood that Jesus shed for us, knowing that he who shows no mercy will be judged in the same way.

There are many in the Body of Christ who have had dreams and visions concerning destruction to the land, and because of that believe it is God's plan. It is time we come to see the dreams and visions as warnings of places where sin has taken place either recently or in the past and that the dreams are meant to lead us so we can pray according to God's heart, not to bring destruction, but grace. Let us consider the examples mentioned above and look at their lives as examples of those who lived in the Old Covenant season among unrighteous nations, but still sought the love and peace of God for the people around them. God told Abraham that he was blessed to be a blessing! How much more are we called to do the greater works as we see the goodness of God unfold in His new covenant of freedom and grace and forgiveness?

The Father is so good to alert us so that we can ask Him for help and direction enabling us to partner with Him to bring healing and restoration. Instead of accepting the dream as a prophecy of certain outcome, we can ask Him for more revelation or, as prompted by the Spirit, learn the history of a place. Then, in partnership with the Lord, forgive those who sinned which shuts the door on the enemy in that particular place so the land can be healed and at peace. Too often multitudes have died because of sin and many of those have lost their opportunity to enter the Kingdom of God, and that isn't His heart or plan. Let us get to know Him and His ways so that we may produce good fruit from noble hearts. Mercy always triumphs over judgement. As sons and daughters of

God He is inviting us to join Him as ambassadors of His Kingdom who walk in the fullness of the inheritance that He has so generously given us.

Reflection Questions

As you read the section on being sons and daughters of the King, what new thoughts stood out to you?

As an exercise for your heart, please write your name below and then make a list of those things that describe you as a son or daughter of God. *For example, my name is Sharon Murphy and I am a royal priest and that means…*

What is one way to apply these descriptions that you wrote of yourself to your life beginning today?

If you have never asked God what your destiny is in Him, or haven't considered it in a while, take some time to ask Him right now. Write down what you sense or hear.

Heart of Worship - Testimonies

Examples and Testimonies

It isn't complicated to bring healing to the place you live and may be as simple as joining a spouse or friend going for a walk on your land or through your neighborhood, asking Jesus to lead the way. Remain in His Presence as you go. Though we hope to help you by giving you guidelines don't let them become a formula. Begin with worship and thanksgiving to our very good Father and for His provision of righteousness, peace, joy, freedom and new life to your home, community, or creation. And as you go, let your heart stay in that place of worship. He has already provided what you need and has given you the ministry of reconciliation. Continue with Him, in intimacy and faith, trusting that He will lead you into all truth and show you His heart and purpose as you go together.

We don't always start out knowing where we are going before we get there, but we continue to abide in the presence of the Lord, worshipping, listening, and following Him and He leads the way. When we get to the location that has been highlighted by the Lord, we partner with our Father staying always dependent on Him because nothing happens without Him. Throughout the book of Joshua as the Lord sent the children of Israel, time and time again He told them that He directed and fought for them. We trust Him to do the same for us.

In *Isaiah 45:2-3* there is a prophetic word that applies to how we pray:

> *I will go before you and make the crooked places straight; I will break in pieces the gates of bronze and cut the bars of iron. I will give you the treasures of darkness and hidden riches of secret places that you may know that I, the Lord, who call you by your name, am the God of Israel.*

The Lord goes before us and we follow Him. These verses have come to life as the Father has made them real to us more than once, by making the way straight and revealing the treasures and the hidden riches He has for us. We do cleanse the land, but that is only a small part. Releasing healing and then decreeing by faith what God has revealed go hand in hand.

Let your heart abide in the place of worship in all that you do. Keep listening, keep asking, seeking, and knocking and keep releasing what you receive! Jesus said that the *words* (*rhema*) that He speaks are Spirit and life. *(John 6:63)* Those are the words that will transform our homes, cities, and nations!!

> *We simply forgive all who have sinned as the Spirit of God directs us. Forgiveness doesn't make sinful actions any less heinous or painful, but it does mean the light of God is now released and spiritual darkness must go*

It is important to forgive all who sinned. For example, in our area the Native American people suffered atrocities because of the sins of the white settlers. They broke covenant with the Native people, killed them, and, through idolatry of self and riches, repeatedly used and abused them, as well as committing sexual acts of immorality against their women and children. There has been much to forgive, and often very specific acts come to light.

On the other hand, many of the Native American tribes practiced idolatry and witchcraft before the white men came and also committed acts of bloodshed, sexual immorality, and broken covenant among each other. Their responses to the white men's sin (whether seemingly justified or even necessary for survival) also included sinful behavior. When people have sinned, it isn't our job to place blame, make excuses for behavior, judge them, or take sides. We simply forgive all who have sinned as the Spirit of God directs us. Forgiveness doesn't make sinful actions any less heinous or painful, but it does mean the light of God is now released and spiritual darkness must go.

As you release forgiveness wait until your spirit witnesses with Holy Spirit that the sins have been forgiven. Sometimes there are more sins than are apparent at the beginning. Just keep in tune with the Lord and wait until He says you are finished.

We don't at any time engage the enemy during this process. It isn't necessary because in forgiving the sin, the enemy no longer has a place and he knows it. We don't get our cues from him, nor try to figure out what he is doing or his strategy, though the Spirit of God may reveal it. We stay with the Lord and what He is doing and remain under the cover of our Father's wings and by forgiving the sin, we enforce the victory of the Cross. Sometimes we aren't absolutely sure what all of the sin is, so there may have even been a few times we forgave sin that someone didn't do but forgiving too much doesn't seem to create a problem.

After releasing forgiveness, we also wash those who sinned and the land with the blood of Jesus for cleansing and redemption, and then healing is released into creation. This is very important because roots of sin cause wounds. When those roots are removed, healing needs to be poured out. Then, as sons and daughters of our Father of blessing, we declare words of life, freedom, and blessing. The Spirit of prophesy often inspires these declarations, establishing the true destiny and calling of the land, city, etc. As the Spirit leads, we ask the Father to send an angel or angels to facilitate, cultivate and protect what we have released. We ask according to the Word in *Hebrews 1:14 NIV*:

> *Are not all angels ministering spirits sent to serve those who will inherit salvation?*

Sometimes a team member will perform a prophetic act in keeping with the Holy Spirit's guidance. When we return to our meeting place, we always end with sharing testimonies of the day and then worship and praise and thanksgiving.

Find what works best for you. Please don't think you can only do this with a team. Praying over the land becomes a lifestyle. No matter what you choose to do and to glean from what is shared here, partner with the Father as you go in faith. Healing the nations is His idea. Remember to worship in all you do. Use the authority God has given you in humility and grace toward those you forgive. Remember, we are not here to accuse, blame or judge, but to forgive and bless, knowing we are still in need of mercy ourselves. His blood cleanses and restores and is still as powerful today as it was when it was first shed. It heals the land as well as us. God has a plan for the place you live, and He will tell you what it is if you ask Him. Declare His intentions, His heart, and His Kingdom. *(Isaiah 49:8)* And be thankful that the angels are here to minister with us and to cultivate and protect what is done by us. Keep inquiring every time something is revealed and you will almost always receive more. Then give thanks in all things!

At times, it is revealed to us that the strength of the land, its gifts and blessings, were held back because of the harm done by sin in the land. When that happens, we ask for those things to be released to be used to bless the Kingdom of God. There is more than one description God has attributed to the place we live, Spokane, Washington. It has been called a city of refuge, city of healing transformation, city of the Father's heart, and city of divine encounter, to name a few. We often receive things that affirm and empower these words. Recently, we learned that long before the city was built by white settlers, prophetic words were given through visions and dreams to the First Nations people here to tell them that white men with black robes were coming who would teach them about God. This stirred a great hunger to know the true God. Many years later, the Jesuits and other missionaries came, and were welcomed by the First Nations. When the opportunity arose for some native boys to be schooled, though it was at a trading post settlement hundreds of miles from home, two chiefs sent their sons. They were gone for several years. One of the boys, who later became chief, Spokane Garry, was the first father of the faith and considered an apostle in our region. He was probably about 18 years old when he returned to the area, and he knew Jesus. He preached the gospel to His people and established churches and a school where he served as pastor and teacher. He functioned as an evangelist to other tribes in the northwest including the Nez Perce and Kalispel. *(For more information on this subject I recommend* One Church, Many Tribes *by Richard Twiss.)*

Later when the white men began to settle in our region, he tried to bring peace and understanding between the European settlers and the tribes. There was much harm done to him through racism and dishonor. Instead of supporting him and finding a way to help him continue in the work of the Kingdom amongst the other tribes, he was pushed aside and disregarded because he wasn't white. He was robbed of his home and possessions later in his life. There were other ways that people sinned against him. The Christians rejected him or, at least, minimalized him. We forgave the sins perpetrated against him and other Native people who had been dehumanized, dishonored, and not seen. We forgave Chief Garry for losing heart and for other sins in his life and demolished the enemy's stronghold. Words of healing and destiny were released, and we sensed a deep honor from the Lord toward our brother, Chief Garry.

We also understood by the Spirit that we received the gift of fathering and the five-fold ministry gifts that God had given Chief Garry but had been rejected by the early Christian leaders who settled here. His many gifts had fallen to the ground and were largely ignored rather than being received and passed on to the generations as part of the legacy that was meant to be here for the Body of Christ. As the spirit of prophecy came upon us as a team, we declared over specific leaders and the Church in our city who we knew had stewarded the presence of the Lord and would use these gifts to continue to build according to the Father's heart. We also released a general word of blessing over those of the five-fold ministry in our area we didn't know (but God knows), that would use the gifts to benefit the Kingdom. Our spirits soared as we bore witness that God had imparted something that had been lost but now was found and would add significantly to the work of the Kingdom of Heaven in our region.

God has shown Himself mighty and gracious time and time again. He leads us and even helps us navigate. We have even been driving down the road and made what we thought was the wrong turn that brought us to the exact place we needed to be!

Over the past few years, we have been in our downtown area quite a bit for prayer assignments and recently we are seeing many of those areas being revitalized. A beautiful park is now in a place that once was dark and defiled. There are older neighborhoods that felt unsafe to walk through even in the daytime that are now becoming lively communities that are attracting families and new businesses.

On one assignment we were led to be open to 'go into the mountains of influence', not quite understanding what it meant. We had been invited to a little town in Idaho by a husband and wife who had more than one business in the area and were following the leading of Holy Spirit as they pursued the Kingdom of God in bringing restoration to the town. They asked us to bring some team members and train some of the believers in the area to do what we do, and also, to pray for their struggling businesses. We met in their restaurant. As we joined together and asked the Father for His leading, He gave a word of knowledge to two people on the land team that someone had been cheated in a business dealing in establishing the town. The business owners were amazed because they knew the history of the town, and their restaurant was one of the first buildings to house a commercial business during the early settlement of the town by the Europeans.

The white man who built it had cheated the Native American people to obtain their land. He had broken his word with the Natives and in doing so had broken covenant with them and sown seeds of mistrust. The husband and wife had not shared this with us, and furthermore they had constantly run into mistrust from the community God had sent them to serve. We forgave the original land/business owner and removed the enemy's illegal access and released the healing and blessing of the Father, restoring the business and land back to the Father's original intent. We followed our Lord into the mountain of business that day.

As part of the training the next day, several groups went out led by Holy Spirit to several places to release the destiny of the land, forgive those who sinned, and cleanse the land. When they returned to debrief, we found out that many sins had been revealed and forgiven, but the main one that was revealed over and over again was broken covenant and the consequent mistrust that had affected many of the townspeople including those in the Body of Christ in the area. A few weeks later the testimony shared with us was that the Church was working together in unity in a much greater way, and that our friends, the business owners, were finding a new acceptance in the area as well as greater success.

Since that time, we have also been directed into other mountains of influence. One of them was the mountain of government (which had nothing to do with politics from our standpoint) but resulted in the election of a new mayor who immediately invited Christian leaders to have influence in his leading of the community. We believe that through removing the influence (due to sin) the enemy has had in these areas, we help to make a greater place of impact for those believers who are called to these various areas of influence, that they might do the greater works of *John 14:12*. *(For more understanding on this particular subject I recommend* The Seven Mountain Mantle *by Johnny Enlow, and* The Seven Mountain Mandate: Impacting Culture Discipling Nations *by Loren Cunningham.)*

Again, it is important to stress that there is no 'normal' in what we do. Each assignment is unique, and we are sometimes surprised by what we find when we go where we are guided by Jesus, our High Priest. On several different occasions we found something we were not looking for: satanic altars. Before we arrived at the particular location the first time we found an altar, we asked Jesus to reveal to us what He was seeing and we saw the sin of witchcraft and some animal sacrifice, but we were still not expecting to find what we did. The other altars were discovered in the same way, simply by following the Lord.

All of them were in places that seemed to be deliberate in spreading defilement: one next to a freeway, some by the river, and yet another next to a local television station. We did the same, simple things on those assignments that we always do; we found out what the root sins were that made a place for this kind of activity and who sinned, and then we forgave those who sinned, cleansing them with the blood of Jesus. The altars were left intact physically, but the enemy's authority and power were cast down by the blood of the Lamb and the word of our testimony, and because we don't love our lives to the death. *(Revelation 12:11)* In staying under the authority and protective wings of our Father, the enemy didn't know what hit him, but the light of the Kingdom shines brighter in our city!

It may be helpful for you to know that in one of the situations described in the previous paragraph, a team member who is especially gifted in seeing and feeling saw and felt the demonic realm manifest as we stepped on the land and it created anxiety for him. At this point it was up to the leader of the group to keep his eyes on Jesus and remain in the rest and peace of the Kingdom, and to remind the team that they were still under cover and to face their God. It could be very distracting or disconcerting if we forget that we are following Jesus and resting in Him as we go.

The enemy would like to scare us or get us to follow his lead and tactics. Instead we trust in our Father and listen so that we know how He wants us to proceed. We focus on what His original intent was for the particular place, and then we simply forgive those who sinned and wash them with the blood of the Lamb. At this point the rights of the enemy are defeated. We release healing into the land and declare prophetic words of destiny and assign angels to guard and nurture those words. The same person who was anxious because of what he had seen and felt then testified that what he was seeing, and sensing was gone and was replaced by the atmosphere of Heaven, the atmosphere that we carry with us!

On another occasion one of the team reported that she was still seeing demonic activity after we had forgiven the sin of an individual who killed many people. We took it as a clue and asked Jesus if we missed something, and He revealed a sin that had been overlooked. After we released forgiveness by our designated authority and cleansed the land with the blood of Jesus, the seer happily announced that the air was clear, too!

There have been assignments that we call pre-emptive strikes, preventative actions that keep destruction from coming on the land. More than once we have been led by Holy Spirit to places where there are fault lines or possible volcanic activity in our state and region to forgive the sins of the people in the past and present, and to forgive those who are prophesying destruction and loss over the land now. When we have released healing and blessing we ask God to assign specific angels to the places He has cleansed and healed, and to establish those things that have been prayed and declared by His sons and daughters, the heirs of salvation. *(Hebrews 1:14)*

In May of 2011, Holy Spirit was highlighting Spokane's aquifer to the team. A couple of weeks before we were to meet, one of the land team felt her bed shake as she was laying there. It went on for a while, but her husband didn't feel anything. It happened again the following night. She asked the Lord about it but wasn't certain what He was saying. While at the Healing Rooms the next day, someone shared that two people on the staff had been having a strange thing happen. Their beds shook when they lay down at night. About this time a team member heard the word 'subduction' which they looked up and found out it has to do with earthquakes. This led to research that considered the possibility of an earthquake near the aquifer.

On the day of the prayer assignment three individuals brought maps. One team member brought a map of the fault lines in our area. Another person brought a map of the aquifer. Yet another, by the leading of the Spirit, but 'knowing it didn't make sense', brought a map/diagram that showed the wall around Jerusalem with the placement of the gates during Nehemiah's time. *(Nehemiah 3)* As we looked at the maps, we realized that it was our first 'preemptive strike'. From comparing them we could see the fault lines ran directly under the aquifer and by overlaying the diagram of the gates we received leading as to where we were to go because there were gates on the Nehemiah map that coincided with the fault lines. Instead of praying after something catastrophic happened, we believe God led us to several places that day where we forgave those who sinned and released healing and the peace of the realm of the Kingdom. Step by step, Father got our attention and led us in the way we should go. We simply followed His lead and did what we saw Him doing and said what we heard Him saying. Creation often responds through a variety of beautiful manifestations as it begins to experience freedom from futility and restoration to its original destiny. That day eagles put on aerial displays more than once, but we have also seen rainbow and cloud formations of unusual shapes and birds bursting into joyous song as creation joyfully receives its healing and joins us in praising our Creator.

One more very important thing before you begin: as has already been stated, this is spiritual warfare so we highly recommend that you, and every person you are going to pray with, are prepared for battle by staying in close relationship with the Father, Son and Holy Spirit. The whole armor of God is worn by those who have presented themselves as a holy, living sacrifice to Him and are allowing Him to transform them into His image from glory to glory. In this place of abiding and rest make sure your heart is whole or in the process of wholeness before the Lord; that you are not harboring unforgiveness; that wounds are healed or healing; and that sin is being dealt with. We are all in a process, but if there is sin that our fathers in the faith would have called besetting (harassing, ongoing, hampering) sin, then it should be dealt with through repentance first.

We use a similar process in praying for each other on the team as we do on the land, making sure that generational sin is dealt with, as well as our own. This simple process may be useful to you. Before a person joins the team, it is required that they have Transformation Prayer. In a group of 3-4 (including the person requesting prayer), we usually start by thanking the Lord for the person before us and what He has already done in their life, then we ask Jesus to reveal if there is anything hindering the person from walking in the fullness of their destiny or the love of God for them. We usually get revelation including pictures or words, memories, etc. We follow Holy Spirit and continue to inquire of Him (and the person receiving prayer) until it is evident who sinned and needs to be forgiven. Most often, we are praying with them more than for them.

We don't go digging, or striving to find something, we simply ask in partnership with the Lord. As sin is uncovered, the person, as a royal priest, gives forgiveness (with authority) to those who sinned and cleanses with the blood of Jesus. Generally, there is more than one person that needs to be forgiven, including the person we are praying for, so Holy Spirit often leads him/her to repentance. We continue abiding and listening and asking questions of the Lord and the one receiving the prayer, and he/she continues to forgive those who sinned. This often takes great courage and grace, which the Father gives. The forgiveness through the blood and authority of Jesus removes the root of the sin so the accuser no longer has any ground to stand on; the others then pour healing into the places where the roots have been removed and declare the truth over the person being prayed for including prophetic words of destiny and blessing. We encourage every team member to stay in an intimate, vulnerable relationship with the Lord in their daily walk and also to get prayer from others occasionally. The growth and fruit in their lives is evident, as they abide in the Vine *(John 15:1)* and it is a great way to stay free and close to their Father. *(see appendix for more)*

And More Testimonies!

Tom and I started leading the Transformation Land Team for the Healing Rooms and, looking back, we realize there have been many positive changes since we have started. We attribute this to the Father's heart for our city as we have partnered with Him and the wonderful prayer team of faithful and gifted people who show up ready and expectant every time we meet, many who have interceded for years for our city. We are also very aware of the many individuals, churches, ministries and service organizations who have been contending for our city and helping the needy for years who have "gone before us" so to speak, in preparation to what we are doing today. All share a part in the fruit we are now seeing, and we want to make sure that is clear, and that our testimony is only in part ours. It belongs to many others, but if they haven't visited some of these places or kept track of the local news, they may not have noticed the changes. Some of the changes are obvious but some need to be spiritually discerned. When we pray for a person, we can ask them how they feel or for a number to describe their pain level, but it doesn't work that way with the land or the city. God does reveal healing and changes in the land if we are paying attention! Before I share some of our testimonies with you, let me share our 'why'.

We really do love the land and we love the place we live, but that isn't really our main reason for what we do. When we pray in our authority, forgiving those who sinned and cleansing and healing the land with the blood of Jesus, the land is no longer defiled. We then release words of life and destiny prophetically over the city or place where we are praying. It is really this simple. As we do this it removes the enemy's access to occupy these places and instead <u>makes more room for the Presence of God and atmosphere of Heaven to reside.</u> So our main reason to do what we do is to make room for more of God's presence in our city, so that His goodness and glory and love will touch the people who live here (and pass through here) and those <u>people will be blessed and transformed.</u>

We have seen things change and one of the things apparent to those of us on the team is that God's presence rejuvenates and that our Father really does want things to be better. That may seem like a no brainer, but from some of the prophetic words we hear it seems important to mention.

In downtown Spokane there are many areas where we have prayed that were dark and defiled at first. It sometimes feels like we are peeling an onion as we go back to some of the same places and Holy Spirit reveals more of our Father's will for a place and then shows what is hindering that will so that we can pray in agreement with Him.

The good news is that it's working and here is a sampling of just a few of the places we have been and some of the changes related to them: in the midst of what many were calling a recession there was growth and life in many parts of Spokane. Especially noticeable to us is that in some of our poorer and high crime neighborhoods where we have prayed, the landscape is changing and there is even a new voice coming out of those neighborhoods saying that change is there for good! One of those neighborhoods used to be 'scary' to walk through in the daytime, but now young families are moving in and it is becoming safer and peaceable. On a walk through there it really did feel like a different place! Our local power company donated some land and created a park in the heart of our city right next to the waterfalls. It's beautiful, but that wasn't always the case. It was also one of the places we had been more than once so imagine our joy when we saw this new park!

The downtown (main) Masonic Temple and four others that we know of have closed. Most had been operating for a very long time.

In 2015, teams that were trained through the Healing Rooms School of Transformation went to some of our public schools. By going on Saturday no one was disturbed by their presence. One high school, Rogers, was highlighted to us. It is in the poorest zip code in the state and had the lowest graduation rate. It was designated a "Failing High School" and *The Seattle Times* had called it a "dropout factory." Just months after praying, it was reported on the news and in the local paper that there has been a complete turnaround at Rogers. As a matter of fact, the title of one newspaper article was *The Rogers Revival!* The graduation rates and school attendance are currently one of the best in our area and it's now an example for other schools and it's reported that the changes in the school are affecting not only the students, but their families and the local community, too. There are still changes that need to come but what an encouraging and hopeful start!

One of the places we have prayed a lot is at the Healing Rooms headquarters and in the surrounding neighborhood, the South University District. After Transformation Prayer, South University Distract experienced a lot of changes when the city council decided to revitalize the area with a $32 million investment. Another amazing account is that a team prayed in the area and addressed the prostitution problem that had long persisted less than a mile from the Healing Rooms offices. A business owner had shared with someone on our team that a neighboring building had one of the earliest brothels in it, and that many of those being trafficked were enslaved. After forgiving those who sinned and releasing healing, a dramatic change has already been noted. A newspaper article came out telling of a new strategy the city used to deal with the prostitution resulting in almost all of the prostitutes willingly leaving our city with no harm done to any of them. There is much, much more happening in our region and city and even beyond, but this isn't meant to convince you that we are doing something, but that God is doing something and that He wants to do it where you live, too.

I Corinthians 15:46 says that the spiritual doesn't come first, but the natural, and after that the spiritual. We are seeing the outcome of God's Kingdom and atmosphere touching our city in the natural, but we are expectantly looking for the spiritual to manifest with true Holy Spirit revival resulting in people saved and healed and their lives changed, and for great peace and joy to manifest as Jesus Christ receives the reward of His suffering, and the earth and all that is in it gives praise to our God and King.

Testimonies 2020

One of the most heartwarming testimonies came while in Uganda. It was September 2017, and a team and I were there to teach about healing of people, and how to partner with God to bring healing transformation to the land. The day after the training, the team and I went out on the land together for many hours and covered much territory from Entebbe to Kampala and back. The first place we stopped was a jinja stone on Lake Victoria. God highlighted the stone to us as we prayed for direction together, then our host explained that it was a place where tribal chiefs would offer human sacrifice to appease the 'snake king' that lived on a nearby island. He also told us that recently there had been many women murdered and dismembered and left on the stone. The police had no leads and thought it might be a serial killer or even a gang of people because there had been so many deaths. When we arrived at the stone there were soldiers guarding the only access road to keep any more murders from taking place. Our host, Pastor Grace, explained to the soldiers that we were missionaries and that we would like to pray for healing for their land and they granted us access. After we parked, we walked over to the large jinja stone that sat on the shore of the lake and we stood on it. Where idolatry, death, and defilement had taken place for generations we immediately felt God's presence and peace surround us. We knew from our Father that this was meant to be a peaceful place where the beauty of Lake Victoria could be enjoyed. We could see Snake Island from where we stood. As a team we simply forgave the chiefs and others who had committed bloodshed, idolatry, sexual immorality, and breaking of covenant with their own people in this place. We also released forgiveness over whoever was currently committing the heinous murders. There were some other things as well, and when we finished forgiving, we washed the jinja stone and Snake Island with the blood of the Lamb and released healing into the land. We then decreed God's original intent over the land and released angels to protect, nurture, and cultivate what had been done there, and we began to walk back to the car.

Before we could get there a rifle-carrying soldier dressed differently than the ones that were guarding the land met us to tell us we could not be there. We were adjacent to the Entebbe Airport and he was part of the security force. Pastor Grace assured him that we were leaving and explained what we had been doing. Then the pastor asked if we could pray for him in anyway. The young man surprised us all by saying, "Yes, please! I need salvation." Pastor Grace led the young man in a prayer for salvation and we had some words of knowledge and encouragement for him. We were thrilled and praised the Lord, our God as He confirmed His word and the healing of the land to us through this immediate fruit. But He wasn't finished.

As we drove through the guard post on our way out of the area, there was only one soldier there. We got out of the car to thank him for allowing us access. After thanking him, the pastor asked if we could pray for him in anyway and he replied, "Yes, I need Jesus in my life." You can imagine our joy as another man met Jesus, received the forgiveness and cleansing of his sin that day, and was born again into the Kingdom of God.

As we got back into the car, Pastor Grace proclaimed, "Revival!" Then he told us he had asked many soldiers over the years if he could pray for them, and their answers were always the same, they asked for a promotion or better wages. We praised God and gave thanks to Holy Spirit for leading us in His way. And it was just the beginning of the day. We prayed over so many places that day that we didn't even stop to eat until late evening and then we headed back to our hotel to pack.

As we rode through what appeared to me to be a poorer neighborhood between Kampala and Entebbe, Uganda, I looked around and realized I didn't see any farm animals or gardens, so I asked the pastor why. He explained the soil wasn't good for farming and, again, I asked why because it looked like rich soil to me. He replied that it was for the very reason he had heard me teach about the day before. He said that there had been so much sin that had defiled their land throughout their nation that when they did plant seeds, they received nothing or very little in return.

As we sat in the airport waiting for our early morning flight to Kenya, Pastor Grace remembered that I had shared that we often see our testimonies in the newspaper, so he went to buy a local paper. It should be said that it doesn't usually happen overnight, but when Pastor Grace returned, he excitedly showed us the front page. There were two sets of headlines on the front page which I found out wasn't normal. Each one addressed something we had prayed over the day before. The first one was about corruption in the government being exposed and dealt with which, before this, had never happened publicly. Then an article revealed that the police were getting ready to arrest the man who had been killing the women at the jinja stone. Two days later we got word that the arrest had been made.

Three years later as I write this, there have been so many wonderful testimonies of God's goodness and we have received wonderful pictures of the gardens that they are growing. Pastor Grace has continued to pray over the land and the healing has not only made it possible to garden, but the transformation is amazing. If this was an illustrated book, you could see pictures of thriving crops such as corn, coffee, cassava, and potatoes that wasn't possible before and, in some cases, they are much larger than normal. I have seen pictures of avocados the size of an American football. It would also show the joy of those who are reaping and sharing the wealth of the land as it is being restored back to its destiny. Now their chickens, pigs, cows, and goats are thriving. Just this year one of their goats gave birth to healthy triplets. There is enough food for their animals. In addition, it has been reported that the land is now cleansed and healed before gospel crusades and there are so many more salvations and healings than had been experienced in the past.

I have received testimonies from one of the pastors in Kenya who went back to his village after the training and forgave his ancestors for their sins and released healing and God's blessings over the village. He contacted me about eight weeks later because he was so excited and grateful for what the Lord was doing in his village and he sent me a picture of the machines that were being used to build the first ever road to his village. About three months later I received another message from the pastor because the village now had a well. Several months passed and I heard from him again saying the best news ever, his father had received salvation through our Lord Jesus Christ!

A pastor from Liberia was also trained. Before the training, he and his wife prayed at their Healing Rooms for many people who would receive healing and then go home but would return to them again for healing prayer with the same sickness. Holy Spirit spoke to them after the Transformation Prayer training and they began to try something new that proved successful. When a guest came to their church for healing prayer they would agree to pray for them but the pastor or other team members would ask if their team could accompany them to their home where they could also pray over their home and land for healing. They discovered that the sickness was at least partly because of the contamination of the sin that was on the land and, after the land was cleansed and healed, there was rarely a need to pray for someone a second time.

A testimony from a prayer team in Morehead, Kentucky, states that Morehead has become a busy place with the addition of new industry and businesses since the team began to pray over their city. One of the places that has received quite a lot of prayer is the University of Morehead, which was recently named the safest campus in the state of Kentucky.

So many of our testimonies have come from being with a team and we highly recommend you pray with others. We all see in part and together we get more parts. Transformation prayer has become a lifestyle for my husband Tom and I. We have prayed over our own land and seen results, and we often pray in this way when various problems arise. When we are travelling, even when on vacation, Holy Spirit almost always leads us to a place that needs God's healing touch, so we simply join with our Father's heart of love for the place we are visiting and pray.

Because I want to encourage you to join in being a part of healing our cities and land, I want to share a testimony that came to me when I was at the Spokane Healing Rooms one day as a part of the team. It was my turn to cover the desk for our receptionist and a stranger approached me. He had overheard someone else talking to me and asked me if I was Sharon Murphy. I said yes and he asked if I was the Sharon Murphy who wrote this book. I admit I was a little embarrassed because others were now listening and team members were chuckling, but I said I was. He was from Montana and many years before he had invited Cal Pierce and a team to come and train them so they could start a Healing Rooms there. The man felt this was a turning point in his life so, after the training, the man asked Cal if he would come to his home and pray. The team went and prayed, and the man planted a tree on his property while they were there as a sign of his commitment to the Lord. In the years that followed the man had a lot of struggles, there were sicknesses, and even deaths of loved ones. It had been challenging to his faith but the thing that finally caused him to be offended was the tree he planted died. He didn't pull it up but every time he would see it, he felt hurt. As he read my book the Holy Spirit spoke to him and he realized he had been offended at the Lord and he shared with me that he repented and then in his authority he forgave himself. He then went outside and prayed over the land and the tree itself. He said it changed his heart and that he was experiencing new life and joy and intimacy with the Lord again! And God gave him a miracle: the tree came back to life. Now every time he looks at that tree, he remembers God's love for him.

Meanwhile back in Spokane, we rejoice because when Holy Spirit leads us to pray over those darker or poorer areas of our city revitalization is the fruit. Just days after we finished an assignment that had taken us into the dark alleys of our downtown core many times, the city planning committee announced its intention to turn the alleys into beautiful parks and marketplaces. You can imagine our joy and worship as God so generously responded to us yet again! Often it feels like Holy Spirit simply sets us up to see what it is God really wants to do. We knew going into the alleys was God's idea, but it is another thing to see the results are beyond simply cleansing and making a safer place for the people who use them. God has good plans.

Another testimony worth sharing is that despite political differences in this divisive election year, our city leaders are working together to bring about reconciliation, prosperity, and safety for the people who live here. In ten years, we have accumulated a file cabinet full of testimonies and we are still in awe of what God is doing and continues to do as we join Him. He is faithful. There have been changes in many other places too and some we may never know about, but we are grateful for the many specific answers and glad to be part of what God is doing to bring His life and love into our region. As it says in the introduction of the book, we are not experts. It has been an amazing journey and God has led us into greater measures of His joy and goodness and I am so very grateful. Today I hope you will decide to join Him and go out there and make a difference in the places you have influence so that the name of our Lord Jesus Christ will be lifted up and He will receive the glory He so truly deserves!

Teamwork

If you feel called to your city or region, you may want to join with other Spirit-filled, like-hearted lovers of God who desire to make a commitment to be part of a body of believers who heal the land.

If you are interested in forming a team wait for the Father's leading. Above all, if the Father isn't going with us, we aren't going. In our Spirit led serving it is God who works. We rest in Him, the all sufficient Father, and He works in us for the glory and honor of His name.

We urge those who want to lead that you seek the Lord's direction with surrendered hearts for Him and His Kingdom. Your own relationship with the Father is going to be crucial as you listen to Him and receive direction for what is on His heart. It's important to have leaders that can follow and are of teachable humble hearts and that have given themselves to serve the King and His Kingdom. True leaders 'see' others and enjoy, honor, and love them. The gifts of the Spirit are necessary and useful in what we do, so a good understanding of how God moves through these gifts is important.

At the same time, it is essential to value the people on the team more than their gifts. One of the ways for this to happen is for the leaders to pray for their team individually and/or corporately. Leader(s) do well to stay dependent on the Lord Jesus and His revelation as they set the teams in place to go out, and then release them to follow Holy Spirit. It is important that leaders have a vision of what God is doing, but it also falls on them to delegate, make sure details are covered, and to make decisions in the field. True leaders not only have a vision, but are genuine visionaries. They see what is needed for today's assignment, and they are far-seeing, moving forward and taking others with them.

Our team meets together occasionally to worship and wait together for direction. As the Father reveals His plans to the group (and when we go out also), the leader needs to hear what each individual has to say and at the same time hear Holy Spirit and help build consensus so that the team also carries the vision. Something that leaders need to remember as they do this is that others may receive words, pictures, etc. from the Lord that are different than what the leader is getting. Hear them! Process them with Holy Spirit. The majority of the time it's as important as what the leaders are hearing and sometimes more so. At times, there may be different perspectives so listen and pray together and let God work in and through all of it. Most of our team members are forerunners and they are strong leaders, so it is important for us to honor them by hearing them and affirming their gifts of leadership that they may receive grace to continue to flourish and be ready to lead with the same grace God gives them. Consistent and stable leaders help build a place where others are safe and inspired to grow into who God created them to be.

On our particular team there is a very wide diversity of gifts, abilities, and individuals; and we love it. There are those on the team who have prophetic gifts in seeing, hearing and feeling. There are those who love the land and have particular wisdom that is rooted in that love. We have fathers and mothers who bring stability to the team. There is a wide diversity of ages, from 18 to 80+. A farmer, grandparents, a biologist, worship leaders, counselors, Charismatics, evangelicals, and a nun are just a small representative of those who join us. At first, it was a little awkward as we made our way, but we each yielded ourselves to Jesus, our Head, and He has generously led us into a greater gift than we expected.

One of the blessings that we have experienced as a team is that we have become a family. As we surrender ourselves to our Father in love and expectancy, He brings increase in individual gifts, and we seem to 'rub off on each other' so that, for example, being with a seer increases another person's ability to see. As we stay in a place of humility, honor, and love toward each other, we increase with the increase of God *(Colossians 2:19)* as a family. It is such a joy!

Usually when we meet as a team we begin with worship and inquire of the Father and wait until He answers. Laying down our agendas and ideas, we exchange them for His. We pray for one another and anoint each other and receive God's covering and protection. Of course, the whole armor of God should always be worn. *(Ephesians 6:10-18)* As Holy Spirit leads through the various gifts of each individual He may be very specific or give just enough to get us moving in a general direction. We hear what He is saying and do what He is doing and, by faith, we follow Him.

Abiding in this place of worship as we go and following Holy Spirit together means there isn't a set way to do things because the Spirit is like the wind and so are we. Holy Spirit will reveal who is to be the leader on each assignment and it is the leader's job to listen to Him and to each member of the team. Everyone has a part and we have found that often those things that may at first seem insignificant can be important. If you have ever worked a large puzzle and lost one piece you can understand the need for each member to bring their part. Going out with a team has been such a blessing in our lives and we believe adds a synergy to our prayers through the unity of the Spirit that we don't experience on our own!

As we stay in a place of humility, honor, and love toward each other, we increase with the increase of God (Colossians 2:19) as a family. It is such a joy!

Reflection Questions

What have you learned that is helpful and will keep you in a safe place as you take part in this kind of warfare?

What is God's intention for the place you live?

How is your home or neighborhood producing fruit for the Kingdom of God?

List the places in your sphere of influence that the Holy Spirit has put on your heart as you have read this manual.

What is the Father saying about those places? What is the calling and is there sin that has allowed the enemy access?

Activation

We recommend that you take a Healing Rooms training before praying on the land. The same principles we practice in healing people are present when healing the land so it would be a good background to have. Healing is an act of faith and it doesn't necessarily manifest the minute it is released. Faith is a seed and sometimes the transformation is instantaneous, but sometimes it takes time. Healing can be like peeling an onion, which is why we stay open to returning to a place. It doesn't happen often, but when it does we know it is the purpose of God for that day.

Are you ready to get started? There is much that needs to be done, but it is so important to stay in step with Holy Spirit always. He will show you where to go, when to go, and who goes where, etc. You really can do this at home, and that is often a good place to begin! As you partner with the Father (have we mentioned that enough?!?) and join together with a friend or team and intercede in this way, you become part of the solution as you fulfill the mandate of Heaven.

Let *Psalm 85* become one of our prayers:

> *Lord, You have been favorable to Your land;*
> *You have brought back the captivity of Jacob.*
> *You have covered the iniquity of Your people;*
> *You have covered all their sins. Selah. You*

have taken away all Your wrath; You have turned from the fierceness of Your anger.

Restore us, O God of our salvation, and cause Your anger toward us to cease. Will You be angry with us forever? Will You prolong Your anger to all generations? Will You not revive us again that Your people may rejoice in You?

Show us Your lovingkindness, Lord, and grant us Your salvation. I will hear what the God the Lord will speak, for He will speak peace to His people and to His saints; but let them not turn back to folly. Surely His salvation is near to those who fear Him, that glory may dwell in our land.

Mercy and truth have met together, righteousness and peace have kissed. Truth shall spring out of the earth, and righteousness shall look down from the earth. Yes, the Lord will give what is good; and our land will yield its increase. Righteousness will go before Him and shall make His footsteps our pathway.

Father, I pray that the person reading this will help to bring about the great commission as they preach the good news to all of creation; that they would simply and humbly bring the Lamb the reward of His suffering as they fulfill the will of God for their life, whatever and however You have purposed in Your heart. That they would preach the good news to the *poor, heal the brokenhearted, proclaim liberty to the captives, and the opening of the prison to those who are bound, to bring comfort and consolation to those who grieve, and to rebuild the old ruins, raise up the former desolations of many generations, and repair the ruined cities. Father, I believe that You want to use this one in their authority as a royal priest to labor with You as You revive, reform and revitalize Your church, and bring about the greatest harvest of the ages. So I ask that You reveal what their part is and then lead them as they partner with You to answer the prayer of our Lord Jesus and of the church throughout the generations, "Your Kingdom come, Your will be done on earth as it is in Heaven" that the kingdoms of this world become the Kingdom of our Lord and of His Christ and He shall reign forever and ever. I bless Your beloved child in Jesus' mighty name. Amen.*

As you have read these pages I hope you have seen that the land and all of creation are in need of healing and transformation and that as a son or daughter of the Creator of the universe He has invited you to co-labor with Him as a royal priest in administering the victory of the Cross. I hope it is evident that if you, as His child, actively seek His heart, His Kingdom and His ways you will bring holy changes to your environment. The atmosphere of Heaven will be opened over your city and people will experience the fruit of God's love around them. As you partner with your Father in transforming the land our King will be glorified.

This is not meant to be the last word on this subject. It is our hope that it serves as an outline that may motivate you to look at it and say, "Hey, I can do that, too!" The spiritual realm is so vast and beyond our human understanding. This is simply an approach that the Lord gave that has helped to bring the land and our region to new levels of freedom. This is a hands-on process that happens in relationship with our Father. So please find out what the Father's heart is for you and then as you abide in His presence you fill in the outline and paint your own picture of what this is to look like in your home, neighborhood, city, region and nation!

Reflection Questions

What is the Father asking you to do next?

Please take some time to really listen to His heart and, in His peace and rest, partner with Him to bring transformation to your world!

Appendix

Included are summaries of our models and suggestions for working together as a team that have helped during trainings. They are meant to be an aid but only as you are led by Holy Spirit.

Transformation Prayer for Land and Cities

1. Begin with worship of our Father and asking Him to reveal His plans and heart for this place; expect words of knowledge, etc. Pray for Holy Spirit to lead and ask for His covering as you go. Keep in mind what you receive but wait to release it until you have cleansed the land.

2. What is hindering His purposes and destiny in this place? The land is defiled by someone's sin and that has given the enemy a place. (*Ephesians 4:27*) The main defilements to your city or land are bloodshed, broken covenant, idolatry, and sexual immorality. We cleanse the land by forgiving in Christ's authority, as a son or daughter, a member of the royal priesthood, saying, "I forgive..." and specifically forgiving the one who sinned, washing in the blood of Jesus. Keep asking, seeking, knocking, and be specific in your forgiveness until everyone is forgiven that has sinned in this place. Often, we begin 3-4 generations in the past and then work toward the present. It can be helpful to know the history of the place, but don't let that limit you. Stay in the Spirit and do only what He is leading. We say: don't try to dig, just join yourself to Him.

3. When finished with all the forgiveness, release healing into the land or place.

4. Now decree and declare according to God's Word and by the Spirit of the Lord, God's original intentions for this place. Bless, bless, bless! Big, big, big! Declare like the royalty you are.

5. Ask the Lord to send angels to nurture and cultivate what was done.

6. Give God praise and glory for what has been done!

Transformation Prayer for People

AS HOLY SPIRIT LEADS!!!!!

IN THE LOVE OF THE FATHER!!!!!

We always ask the Father how He sees the client and who He created them to be before we bring them into the prayer session. This helps us to see them as He does. We ask the Lord for anything He wants to reveal to us before we bring them into the room.

Once we bring them into the prayer room:

Sometimes it may seem obvious to the client or the team what needs prayer, but we always ask Holy Spirit so that we don't go outside of what God wants to do. We may even start by asking the person if the Lord has revealed anything to them before they came to the appointment. God is going to lead us as we ask Him and if we stay dependent on His leading for what He has for them today.

As we begin praying, we give praise and thanks for the person then ask the Lord to reveal what He wants to them (us), we pause to listen. We will ask the person with whom we are praying what it is they are experiencing, seeing, or hearing, and what it means to them. It may be a memory or an impression. It is okay if they say they are not seeing or hearing anything. Sometimes we wait a little longer. One of the team members may be hearing something that Holy Spirit wants them to mention. The team members should be sensitive to Holy Spirit as to God's timing and interpretation and application of what they are getting. We sometimes ask, "Lord, will You reveal why the enemy has had access in this area?" or "Show us the root of anything that is hindering them from walking in the fulness of where you want them today" or any other specific question that we want the answer to. **Stay in the asking/receiving mode rather than thinking or trying to figure it out**. The answer may be specific sins that may include, but not limited to, generational sins, traumatic events, and unforgiveness. There are **four main areas of defilement** that allow the enemy access - they are: **idolatry, sexual immorality, bloodshed, and broken covenant**.

A key to breakthrough is for the person to forgive whosoever sinned, in their authority as a king and priest. One of the **keys** we have discovered for breakthrough is going beyond personal forgiveness to **priestly forgiveness**. If the person you are praying with is a believer, a simple explanation of our **authority as priests** beforehand should position them to know they are praying and forgiving in the priestly authority the Father has given them. Part of the commission and authority Jesus gave us is to forgive "whosoever" of their sin. (Read *John 20:21-23; Hebrews 7:25; I Peter 2:5-9; Revelation 1:6, 5:10, 20:6; Matthew 9:1-8*)

As particular sins are revealed, ask the person (as a royal priest) to **forgive** their own root sins (in self), **by the blood of the Lamb.** (Hebrews 9:22). Then ask him/her to **repent** of, and **renounce** sinful behavior. Now, if necessary, lead in a prayer of forgiveness to any who wounded or sinned against them that influenced behavior in their own life. Many times a sin may be revealed that goes back generations and those who sinned need to be forgiven so the whole root will be removed. Forgiving generationally is important as the scripture mentions visiting the iniquity of the fathers to the third and fourth generation. (Exodus 34:7) We are removing roots, not breaking things off. We are not blaming anyone, just forgiving whoever sinned. People's sin allows the enemy access to their lives. Priestly forgiveness closes the door that was opened because of the sin.

Some people will be able to pray this on their own with little prompting while others may need you to prompt them through the whole prayer. Either way, it is important to have *them* speak the words.

Very important: Once we know that the roots are removed, we declare those forgiven washed in the blood of Jesus. We pour in healing prayer and release blessings! Look for treasures and declare them! Release the prophetic word per Holy Spirit and declare their new condition. Give thanks for what God has done!!

Suggestions:

If there seems to be a block getting started, these are questions that may help, but only as led by the Spirit:

1) Is there a recurring area of pain, woundedness, or etc., in your life that you know you have forgiven, but it still seems to affect you? (The solution is to instruct them to forgive, not just on a personal level, but as a royal priest.)

2) Is there a history of defilement in your family? (bloodshed, broken covenant, idolatry, sexual immorality)

3) Is there a history of witchcraft in your family? (Freemasonry, Mormonism, pagan, etc.)

Depending on mindsets that have been dealt with, we sometimes caution a client that the enemy may lie and try to convince them that nothing has changed or will try to bring things back that they have already released forgiveness over. We encourage them to cast the liar away from them and stand firm in faith concerning the work the Lord has done.

* This is a guideline, so we encourage you not to do this by rote but stay in a place of asking, listening, and follow His lead!

Team Dynamics - Guidelines

Our primary goal is to go with what God is doing today by laying down everything and walking with Him by asking and receiving, hearing what your team is getting, and in faith speaking and doing what He shows us.

Each team will usually have a leader who is appointed and anointed for the assignment that day to oversee and keep the focus on the God-given assignment and to encourage each team member. Sometimes the team leader may ask those who have not contributed what they are getting. Sometimes they need to redirect some who may be getting off track. Sensitivity to Holy Spirit is important because at times what appears to be a rabbit trail is exactly where God is leading. Also, the leader may guide in asking questions of the Lord out loud at times so our direction continues to come from Him rather than relying on anything else. Usually one person takes notes.

Things to remember:

- Each team stays together. No one wanders off.
- We start with finding out the destiny (the GOLD) God has created the place for. He will tell you when you ask.

- Ask what is preventing that from happening (ask for the root of who sinned that gave the enemy access).

- Stay in a posture of walking with Him by listening, asking/receiving, not relying on our own opinions. (*Proverbs 3:5*) Share what you are seeing and hearing. Some of us have gifts that see what the devil is doing. Don't let that distract you. Just ask why it's there and deal with it.

- Stay on track and be mindful that God has a specific mission today. Stay within His mission.

- The smallest things can be the biggest key.

- We are not engaging the enemy! (breaking off, coming against, etc..)

- As the sins are made evident that gave the enemy a foothold, in your authority as royal priests, forgive those who sinned and declare them washed in the blood of Jesus.

- Remember! We are safe under His wing as we go with Him. We are protected.

- The team leader at times will need to decide something. Please defer to them if that happens.

- Once you know you are finished forgiving those who sinned and cleanse them in the blood of Jesus, then we move into releasing the healing and blessing to fill the void where the roots were.

What that may look like:

- Declare the enemy no longer has a foothold. Declare God's Kingdom come!

- Declare what is, based on the destiny God revealed and reveals. (Revisit the GOLD on your list)

- Declare and release healing into the land.

- Release and declare prophetically what God is saying. Declare blessing etc…

- Release angels to facilitate securing, nurturing, protecting the place *per Holy Spirit*.

When we are finished on the land, we gather at our meeting place with other teams and debrief, celebrating and praising God for what has been done. We release a prayer of forgiveness and cleansing over the team members to cover us if anyone missed the mark during the day.

Other Materials Available from Sharon Murphy

Transforming the Land and Cities on DVD

Visit the bookstore at www.healingrooms.com

Tom and Sharon would be delighted to hear testimonies of your experiences in transforming the land. If you are interested in a training to help establish a team in your area, Sharon is available in person or via Zoom and can be contacted at landteam444@gmail.com.

Printed in Great Britain
by Amazon